If you can collaborate and have people own the results rather than dictating the change to them, you'll be more successful.

Michelle McKenna, Senior VP/Chief Information Officer,
National Football League

Bold, practical, engaging…an inspiring, transformative resource for women leaders.

Shaunti Feldhahn, bestselling author of *For Women Only*
and *The Male Factor*

As an avid reader, there are few books that can really stick with me for a long period of time. You will find yourself excited, determined, and in total agreement with all Deborah's time-tested personal examples as a successful leader and God-fearing woman. Get one for yourself and sow another copy in another woman's life!

Marilyn Hickey, Founder, Marilyn Hickey Ministries, Inc.
Co-host of *Today with Marilyn & Sarah*
Author of *It's Not Over Until You Win*

Smart, sophisticated, spiritual, simple, and straightforward. Deborah Smith Pegues gets it all in *Lead Like a Woman*.

Dr. Leith Anderson, author of *Leadership That Works*
President Emeritus, National Association of Evangelicals

In *Lead Like a Woman*, Deborah Smith Pegues challenges women to pursue their calling with confidence. Every woman in a place of authority or influence will find personal and professional enlightenment in this impactful resource.

Shirley Hoogstra, J.D.
President, Council for Christian Colleges and Universities

Deborah's wisdom is priceless. Many of the recommendations she puts forth are not found in college and business school curricula—leaving many women to learn by trial and error. *Lead Like a Woman* is unbiased, practical, and guaranteed to yield synergistic results when followed. I highly recommend this book to women leaders at every level of authority and to the many men who are committed to seeing them succeed.

Bishop Edward Smith
Presiding Bishop, ZOE Association International
Author of *Fruitfulness: Seven Secrets to Getting More Out of Life*

Lead Like a Woman is a leadership bible for women. Keep it near your desk, underline it, and mark it up because you'll be referring to it again and again. I've always been a huge fan of Deborah's books, but this is an amazing achievement.

Kathleen Cooke
Co-founder & Executive Vice President,
Cooke Media Group and The Influence Lab
Author of *Hope 4 Today: Stay Connected to God in a Distracted Culture*

Deborah has a fantastic way of making truths practical to our daily living and *Lead Like a Woman* applies her amazing wisdom for women in all walks of life. Read this and be inspired and encouraged!

Sarah Bowling
Founder/CEO, Saving Moses, Inc.
Co-host of *Today with Marilyn & Sarah*

Deborah is an absolute pro! This book is a must read for any woman trying to increase her influence. Leadership is a learnable skill and *Lead Like a Woman* has keys that will help you unlock your leadership future.

Chris Robinson, Executive VP, The John Maxwell Team

LEAD
LIKE A
WOMAN

DEBORAH SMITH PEGUES

HARVEST HOUSE PUBLISHERS
EUGENE, OREGON

Cover design by Bryce Williamson

For bulk, special sales, or ministry purchases, please call 1-800-547-8979.
Email: Customerservice@hhpbooks.com

Lead Like a Woman
Copyright © 2020 by Deborah Smith Pegues
Published by Harvest House Publishers
Eugene, Oregon 97408
www.harvesthousepublishers.com

ISBN 978-0-7369-8261-0 (pbk)
ISBN 978-0-7369-8015-9 (hardcover)
ISBN 978-0-7369-8016-6 (eBook)

Library of Congress Cataloging-in-Publication Data is on file at the Library of Congress, Washington, DC.

Printed in the United States of America

20 21 22 23 24 25 26 27 28 / VP-CD / 10 9 8 7 6 5 4 3 2 1

To all women who lead or influence others

CONTENTS

PROLOGUE

"It's a girl!"

From the moment you were born, gender socialization began. Socialization, the process by which we learn how to behave based on societal norms and values, is the basis for the gender stereotypes that you must deal with for the rest of your life. Socialization starts with your parents and is perpetuated by relatives, teachers, and other influencers, who reinforce the different expectations for female versus male roles.

Girls are socialized to embrace pink, be caring and nice, use their "indoor voice," be humble, get along with others, and be "ladylike," as defined by the culture. Boys are socialized to choose blue, be assertive, not cry, and compete to win. Later in life, a problem develops when women aspire or are called to a leadership role.

For centuries, we have been socialized to view leadership as a man's domain. Women who have entered this sacred realm face a double bind: maintaining their femininity while skillfully crossing the stereotype line and being assertive and strong. For some people, both men and women, the idea of a powerful female is still too much to accept as a norm. But things are changing, albeit slowly.

Over the past four decades, the increase in female leaders has produced new approaches to the exercise of leadership. Women's leadership styles have been shown to be more transformative, participative, and inclusive than the leadership styles of their male counterparts.

According to the results of a 2008 Pew Research initiative studying whether men or women make better leaders, participants stated that women possessed the top eight leadership characteristics, including honesty and intelligence, by a ratio of five to one when compared to participants' rating of men.[1]

But despite accounting for nearly half of the workforce in the United States—and more than half of the middle-management positions—women are still rare among CEOs of the largest corporations. In 2019, they held only 5 percent of the top spots at S&P 500 companies (the 500 largest corporations listed on the New York Stock Exchange).[2] According to the World Economic Forum's December 2018 report, it will take another 200 years to close the gender gap at work on a worldwide basis.

These statistics and conclusions are dismal. However, God forbid that you roll over and accept such gloomy pronouncements. You must believe that you are going to be the exception to the predictions of such a deferred outcome. You can't wait 200 years. The good news is that there are some strategies that you can begin to employ now that can fast-track your journey.

Now, just to be clear, this book will not promote a "down-with-men-up-with-women" theme. To do so would be like saying, "Down with my left hand, up with my right." It would be unwise to exclude half of God's creation in managing the business, political, social, or other aspects of his great universe. From the beginning, God instructed man and woman to function as equal, interdependent partners. In Genesis 1:28 (NKJV), God "said to *them*, 'Be fruitful and multiply; fill the earth and subdue it.'" Neither Adam nor Eve could achieve this mandate independently of each other. They were going to have to work together. This was the grand plan not just in the context of marriage but in the operation of the planet. Despite what you have read, heard, or experienced in society and religion, know that men and women can only be "fruitful" (*producing good results or being profitable*) when they work together. Yes, the sexes are different in their design and qualities, but they must begin to see their differences as complementary rather than conflicting. Unfortunately, the first couple ignored the grand plan and the battle of the sexes began.

In the chapters that follow, I will occasionally note the differences between leadership traits in men and women and the winning traits women innately possess. My goal in making these observations is not to be divisive or to exalt women above men but rather to appreciate the differences between them and to show the importance of having both genders represented at the table for maximum productivity and profitability.

There are two things I ask you to keep in mind as we start our journey:

1. At no time is it my intention to paint an entire gender with one broad brush. When I say "Women do this" or "Men do that," I mean *generally*. Neither gender is one big homogeneous group; individual behaviors and exceptions abound on both sides.

2. This book is written with a faith bent and thus reflects my high regard for ancient wisdom (aka the Holy Scriptures). While I've kept references to them to a minimum, I believe the Bible is the best leadership book ever written. Faith is one of my "leading" traits, and I hope my personal experiences and lessons learned and those of the exceptional women leaders I interviewed will inspire you to "cross the stereotype line" and wisely pursue your God-given destiny.

For those of you who are aspiring or new to leadership or those who have not gotten the desired response to your leadership efforts, Part 1 will help you appreciate, embrace, and manage 12 powerful, inherent, and stereotypically female traits that give you an edge as a leader in today's culture. If you have unwisely suppressed them or taken them to the extreme hoping to be more effective, each chapter will challenge you to change your thinking and to avoid turning these assets into liabilities.

Part 2 will highlight 12 counterproductive habits and tendencies that thwart your progress as a female leader. The good news is that you can overcome them all. So if you are ready to look in the mirror, be honest, and commit to making the necessary adjustments, I assure you that you can begin to enjoy a fulfilling, balanced, and prosperous adventure as a woman of influence for such a time as this.

Let's get started.

Part 1

INHERENT TRAITS TO EMBRACE AND MANAGE

COLLABORATIVE:
Experiencing the Rewards of Collective Brain Power

None of us is as smart as all of us.

—Kenneth Blanchard, management guru and
author of *The One Minute Manager*

Most women are natural collaborators; we love relating to people. Collaborating establishes community, validates the worth of others, and can work wonders in our personal and professional lives. I've seen members of my family, as well as former employees, perk up when I simply asked their opinion on an issue. Soliciting someone's input says, "Your ideas matter. You matter." Sharing your wisdom says, "I care about what you care about." Such actions meet one of the basic needs of every human being—the need to belong. Therefore, female leaders can boldly bring this trait to the table because it's been proven that it works. Most women leaders embrace the ancient proverb "In the multitude of counselors *there is* safety" (Proverbs 11:14 NKJV). If future-trend experts are correct, being collaborative will continue to be one of the top leadership skills required for effectiveness and profitability as organizations become more diverse.

Unfortunately, some women see collaborating as a sign of weakness. They believe it makes them appear incapable of making an independent decision. Women are especially prone to not collaborating when they work in a predominately male-dominated industry or environment. They feel they need to adopt a more masculine style—to be that strong, decisive leader who sports a "Lone Rangerette" badge and solves all problems single-handedly without input from others. If that is your mind-set, you are missing out on the different perspectives, the excellence, the respect, and the fulfillment that come when you simply open the door for sharing and receiving knowledge and resources. To reject collaboration is to welcome failure.

_____

To reject collaboration is to welcome failure.

_____

Collaborating to Increase Creativity and Productivity

My first experience in collaborating happened several decades ago when I was working on my master's degree in business administration (MBA) at the University of Southern California. There were very few women in the program, and I was determined to "outshine" the men. One of the courses in the curriculum, Corporate Gamesmanship, required that we work with a professor-assigned team for the entire semester. Each student's final grade would be based on the group's performance. We were charged with running all aspects of a mock manufacturing company. At first, I hated the team approach. I knew *I* was going to work hard, but I did not like the idea that my grade would be based on our collective performance. What if a teammate turned out to be a slacker and didn't hold up his end of the assignments? I was accustomed to striving to be the "star student." This arrangement wasn't going to allow for "stars." After a few days of fuming and fretting, I resigned myself to the reality that we would have to work together, perform our assigned roles with excellence, be flexible regarding team meeting dates and times outside of class, and adapt to other circumstances if we were going to succeed. While the team was diverse in its makeup, our goal was singular: to earn an *A* by running an exemplary company.

Years later, I reflected on the valuable lesson I learned in the class as a result of pooling our efforts, education, and experiences. Our collaboration produced incredible creativity and productivity. Not one team member focused on "shining" individually. We assumed specific roles and responsibilities based on our strengths. The "CEO" of the mock company kept us accountable and focused on our goal. As chief financial officer, I made sure we managed our cash flow without having to get emergency working capital loans when sales plummeted. I was also responsible for maximizing our bottom line. The marketing, manufacturing, and human resources chiefs all fell into step. We each brought the same mind-set to the table. Consequently, our group won first place in the class competition for the best-managed company.

I was reminded of that class experience years later during a corporate team-building exercise. The presenter placed a water goblet on several tables with 10 participants per table. He asked each of us to list (without collaborating with our tablemates) various ways the goblet could be used. We had approximately three minutes to complete the assignment. Someone—not I—won a prize for listing the highest number of uses. The next phase of the exercise was for us to combine our lists and collaborate for even more possible uses. Now the tablemates were not competing against each other; rather, everyone was focused on putting forth ways to expand the uses of the goblet. The results were amazing. From "cotton-ball holder" to "biscuit-dough cutter," we developed an incredible number of ways to put that goblet to work. Management guru Kenneth Blanchard, author of *The One Minute Manager*, was right: none of us was as smart as all of us. Without a doubt, we were better together. Looking back on that experience, I also realized the value of my being there as a female contributor to give a broader perspective based on my experiences. I mean, it was unlikely that a man would think of "biscuit-dough cutter." Fortunately, I had used a glass for such a purpose when I used to help my mother out in the kitchen during my childhood years.

Collaborating to Eliminate Silos

Even though the powerful results of collaborating are well documented, the "silo mentality" is still alive and well in many organizations. Silos are departments that function separately from other departments within an entity rather than as a cohesive group. They pursue their own missions apart from the greater organization. You've seen them. In church, it may be the much-praised choir that will not cooperate with the evangelism department—or any other department whose ministry would be enhanced by the availability of music. In the workplace, we find marketing departments operating independently of the production department. Turf wars between departments competing for resources or recognition abound, with self-sufficient departments refusing to share with or seek support from others outside their function. Left unchecked, such departments can become islands unto themselves as animosity between them and other departments grows, and the organization can become increasingly ineffective. We can blame technology, lack of emotional intelligence, employees' general unwillingness to work together, or any other number of reasons for such a situation. But the truth is that silos are ultimately an executive leadership problem. They exist because they are led by people with silo mentalities. However, when you lead like a woman, you use your natural propensity to collaborate to monitor your own motivations to avoid such organizational disconnection.

Want to know if you have a silo or collaborator mentality? Why not pause right now and ponder the following questions to see if your behavior is in alignment with a collaborator mentality?

- Do you keep the mission of your organization at the forefront of your thinking so that your plans stay in alignment with its overall goals?

- When developing plans for your department, do you stop first to consider how they may impact the finances or manpower of the organization as a whole?

- Do you seek informal or formal opportunities (lunches, events, etc.) to interact with other department heads to understand the goals and operations of their departments and how your department may be able to ease some of their challenges? And vice versa?

If you answered no to any of these questions, maybe it's time to employ your natural collaboration skills to put a stop to your silo thinking. Change starts with the executive leadership team establishing collaboration as a core value of the organization. Even if you are not the chief executive officer, consider ways to implement or improve cross-departmental collaborations within your realm of influence. Why not go as far as evaluating collaboration as part of a manager's or supervisors' performance review? Go beyond lip service and put systems in place that require or reward collaboration.

If you are a ministry or nonprofit organization leader, the same principles apply. How are you faring in your collaboration? Do you reach out to other churches or charities and show support for their programs? Do you attempt to collaborate on ways to enhance the community? Or do you view other organizations as competitors?

One of my ministry clients has a great reputation for supporting other charities. Once, when they received a letter from a struggling nonprofit requesting help to sustain a historic religious house they owned, my client responded with a commitment for monthly support. A few years later, the ailing founder of the charity deeded the highly valued property to my client. He noted, "Of all the organizations we reached out to, this was the only ministry that responded. Therefore, they are the only ones I'd trust to carry on the legacy of this place." The historic house has been upgraded and thousands of visitors pour through its doors each year to commemorate the famed Azusa Street Revival that launched the birth of the Pentecostal movement in the United States. To boot, the market value of the Los Angeles–based property has gone through the roof.

When I interviewed Michelle McKenna, chief information officer for the National Football League, she shared her experience of collaborating in her exciting environment:

Me: Michelle, I love the fact that you are one of the few C-suite women in the male-dominated sports industry. What traditionally female trait do you find that you use most often?

Michelle: Being collaborative. There is more than one way to get results. I don't have a big need to get public praise for how work gets done. I enjoy pulling people together and really driving change in an organization. I know that change is not comfortable for people. If you can collaborate and have people own the results rather than dictating the change to them, you'll be more successful. Plus, I get more satisfaction out of that. I think women are a bit more naturally collaborative. If you can play that strength trait up, it can be very helpful.

Collaborating Inclusively

While you may be a natural collaborator, you must be careful to broaden the base of those you interact with. It is not enough to collaborate with people in your circle of familiarity. You must collaborate *inclusively*—that is, without regard to age, gender, race, economic status, political persuasion, or other demographics. Yes, you must even learn to collaborate with those who (respectfully) oppose your stance on certain issues. However, before you can commit to collaborating inclusively, you may need to engage in a "personal attitude audit." Be honest about how you really feel as you answer these questions:

- Do I really believe that *everyone* brings *something* of value to the table?
- Am I ready to admit and let go of my own biases about certain groups of people?

• Am I willing to defend the concept of inclusion within my organization?

Collaborating via Brainstorming

New perspectives are often facilitated by free-flowing brainstorming sessions. Wise women learn to conduct them like pros. They set the stage by letting everyone know that all ideas will be considered. They never, ever shoot down anybody's idea—no matter how off-the-wall it may sound. They keep the input coming by simply responding, "Thank you for your input," "We will take that under consideration," or "That's an idea." Remember that in brainstorming sessions, a leader's "shoot-down" may result in a participant's shutdown.

The Dangers of Overcollaborating

Since women tend to be communal, there is always a danger in becoming too dependent on the voices of others to validate their decisions. Part of leading like a woman is knowing when it's time to make a courageous executive decision rather than trying to get consensus. There will come a time when you must make a hard decision, whether others agree or not. Such decisions often center on doing the right thing, such as being fair, walking in integrity, and meeting other challenges to your core values and convictions.

You will also need to curtail your collaborative activities when you find yourself overloaded as a result of them. Studies show that the lion's share of collaborative work tends to fall on women. Because we are stereotyped as communal, we are expected to help others with heavy workloads, provide mentoring and training to junior colleagues, recruit new hires, and attend optional meetings. As a result, the evidence shows, women experience greater emotional exhaustion than men. One important solution to this problem is for companies to encourage women to invest different types of resources in collaboration. In 2013, the *Huffington Post,* in partnership with market research firm YouGov, conducted an American poll that looked at the different ways that men and women help others. The results showed that men (59 percent) led in sharing knowledge and expertise versus 39 percent of the women. However, when it came to offering help to others in need, women led the poll with 53 percent doing so versus 32 percent of the men.[1] Clearly, offering help is a lot more labor intensive and time consuming. Thus, if not managed, such efforts can easily result in exhaustion.

Yes, ladies, bring your inherent trait of being collaborative to the table, but never stop learning ways to manage it and not use it to your detriment.

EMOTIONALLY SAVVY:
Controlling Your Feelings, Perceiving Theirs

*When you hire a hand, it comes with
a head and a heart attached.*

—Peter Drucker, management consultant

Emotions are a constant companion on our personal and professional journeys. They have been at the root of great triumphs and great tragedies in families, businesses, governments, sports, and other segments of society. Many people believe that emotions have no place in leadership. However, when you decide to lead like a woman, you embrace the gift of emotions. You learn to manage the ones that advance your ball down the court and to control those that thwart your progress. You also learn to respond to the emotions of others in a productive way.

Risto Siilasmaa, chairman of the Nokia Corporation, believes it is time to pay more attention to emotions. "It's tempting to want to dismiss emotions and insist on making decisions on a purely rational basis. Tempting—but not realistic. We're not robots, and our reasoning is naturally affected by our emotions, especially when the stakes are high."[1] He is crusading for male and female leaders to change the culture of their organizations by encouraging employees to express their emotions without fear of judgment or penalty. I applaud his efforts. However, the centuries-old cultural narrative of the emotional female and the rational male will likely persist for years to come. Some women attempt to counter this stereotype by becoming cold and impersonal in their leadership roles. This strategy usually does not work; it only leads to more stereotyping and hinders their effectiveness.

Numerous scientific studies have shown that women have a greater capacity for emotional expression than men. Notwithstanding, women are not alone in having their negative or positive emotions influence their behavior. Consider King Saul. It was his feelings of insecurity that drove him to make many attempts to kill David, the young shepherd boy who beheaded Goliath the giant after he slew him with his slingshot. Goliath had intimidated King Saul's army for 40 days with his taunts. It was David's heartfelt respect for the king as God's anointed servant and his love for God that kept him from retaliating against King Saul when he had an opportunity to kill him during a vulnerable moment in a cave.[2]

Embracing and Managing Negative Emotions

Emotions motivate us. Sometimes wisely, sometimes unwisely. Even though emotions are our ever-present companions, we must be careful to keep them out of the driver's seat. Opposing our best efforts to stay in control, emotions can often function like my GPS during bad weather conditions—prone to getting the directions wrong and leading us down the wrong path. The commands can be persistent: "Take the next exit" (unaware of the fact that you are on a special fast-track speedway and not in the normal flow of traffic); "You have arrived" (you see no sign of your destination; the clouds have confused the satellite signal). Similarly, emotions can be unreliable. Thus wise women do not put their trust in them. Rather, they analyze them, peeling the "why" onion to get to the core motivation of their behavior.

A woman's emotional savvy may be one of the biggest contributing factors to her professional success. To lead effectively, smart women know the importance of being "emotionally objective" about their feelings. Being so involves a level of honesty that some may have trained themselves to avoid in order to maintain a stiff upper lip or to protect their Teflon image that says, "Nothing bothers me or sticks to me." The reality is that no one can put their emotions in a mental safe-deposit box and deny themselves access to it.

Let's look at a couple of instances where women leaders often find themselves having to engage the gift of being emotionally savvy.

Anger

In my book *30 Days to Taming Your Anger*, I assert that anger is a *secondary* emotion, a protest on behalf of a *primary* emotion. For example, feeling disrespected, dismissed, discriminated against, or disadvantaged will likely lead anyone to feel angry. The women in leadership whom I interviewed and others whom I've observed over the years were wise enough to identify the primary negative emotions internally and later address the situation with the perpetrator or higher authority in a calm and constructive manner. Their self-talk included questions such as "What am I really feeling and what do I want done about it?"; "Is this situation worth confronting or reporting to avoid a repetition or escalation of it in the future?"; "Am I being objective or am I responding to a similar painful experience in the past?" Emotionally savvy women understand that if they are going to address an issue, they'd better be certain about the facts—or risk losing credibility and respect.

> Emotionally savvy women understand that if they are going to address an issue, they'd better be certain about the facts— or risk losing credibility and respect.

When I graduated from college in 1972, my first job was with the Atlantic Richfield Oil Company. I was the first and only female on the internal audit team. Somewhat awed at the novelty of having a woman aboard, my male colleagues would often introduce me to other departments as "our female auditor." I would seethe with anger each time they would say that. Wasn't it obvious that I was a female? I never let them know that I was offended by their behavior. I decided that I didn't want to die on that hill by being labeled supersensitive. I would often play it off jokingly with a curtsy (Shirley Temple–style) and a smile. I overlooked their ignorance and chose to embrace the proverb, "A person's wisdom yields patience; it is to one's glory to overlook an offense."[3] In retrospect, I should have lightheartedly reminded them the first time it occurred that it was an unnecessary part of the introduction. I've become a firm believer in confronting a situation the first time or no later than the second time it occurs. You risk losing momentum and maybe even some respect by keeping silent too long. We are always teaching people how to treat us by what we tolerate.

Most women are adept at delaying an expression of their negative feelings until an opportune time. When consumed with anger, this is indeed the time to embrace and manage that skill until you can deal with the situation calmly. Caution: It's one thing not to respond immediately to your anger but another to bury it. Burying anger is detrimental to your emotional, relational, and spiritual health, so be smart and intentional in addressing a situation in a timely manner. You may find it helpful to write out your script or to rehearse your delivery before confronting a perpetrator or taking an issue to a higher level of authority. Also, seeking counsel from a trusted friend or mentor regarding your choice of words will prove invaluable. Most of all, seek God's guidance. Imagine yourself delivering his approved words with grace, composure, and boldness.

Frustration/Disappointment

Emotionally savvy women control their emotions when something or someone has hindered their progress in achieving a *goal* or *meeting an expectation*. If there seems to be no short-term solution to the problem, they continue to do their jobs effectively without adopting a negative attitude. They know that frustrating people or circumstances are inevitable. They take stock of the situation and quickly assess whether a solution is within or beyond the realm of their influence. In controllable situations, they exercise courage by taking the necessary actions to address or eliminate the frustration (confronting the offender, seeking another job, setting new boundaries with appropriate consequences, disconnecting from toxic relationships, etc.). Now, there are times that they must reevaluate their expectations and consider if they are being inflexible or unreasonable. Since many of us are prone to having a long list of "shoulds" for ourselves and others, we would be wise to seek objective input from trusted friends and mentors.

For uncontrollable situations, the sooner you acknowledge and accept your limitations, the sooner you can give up struggling to do what only God can do. Meditate on Scriptures that emphasize the perfect wisdom and timing of God. Ask for his strength to accept his plan and his timetable, and remember that nobody can thwart your purpose.

To Cry or Not to Cry

Anger, frustration, disappointment, and other negative emotions will often evoke a physical response—the urge to cry. This is where the slope becomes very slippery. Emerging schools of thought say that organizations should move toward accepting crying as a normal expression for women and men. However, most of the men that I interviewed for this book felt crying in a professional setting is the kiss of death for the female leader.

When I interviewed Chris Robinson—a seasoned sales trainer and head of faculty for the John Maxwell Group, the international leadership development firm—he related his experience in dealing with women who cry:

Chris: This is just locker room talk, but I have heard men say that they don't want to work with women because they are too emotional. Of course, my experience is that men are just as emotional, but they express it in different ways. Once, my sales team was tasked with meeting with "Muriel," a female executive who was known for being emotional. You could feel the dread and apprehension among the male team members even before the meeting started. Sure enough, the meeting had only been in session a short time before Muriel started bawling about a certain situation. It made the team very uncomfortable.

Me: So how did you respond?

Chris: I simply tried to create a safe space for her to get to the core of the problem. I let her know that she could be totally honest about the troublesome issue and that she would not be judged. Our goal was to get the facts so that we could deal with the problem and get beyond it.

While Chris had a great mind-set about the crying, it is not yet the norm. If you cry, you risk being perceived as weak, immature, unprofessional, manipulative, or otherwise "not ready" for a prime position. Every woman would be wise to develop a personal coping and countering strategy for when she senses the dam is about to break. Here are a few suggestions that have worked for me:

- Discreetly take a few deep breaths (inhaling seven to ten seconds through the nose and taking an equal amount of time to exhale). I have found this to be effective in very tense situations, especially when I was bordering on feeling powerless or hopeless.

- Remind yourself of the skills and experience you bring to the table, that you are excellent at your work no matter what someone else may think, and that you are called to do it for an appointed time until your season is up.

- Acknowledge your Always-Present Comforter standing right beside you to strengthen you through the ordeal.

- If you are not able to stop the tears, stay powerful by putting them in perspective. Once you have regained composure, state matter-of-factly, "You can see that I feel pretty strongly about this."

Discerning and Responding to the Emotions of Others

Being emotionally savvy involves not only embracing and managing your emotions but also responding to the pain, adversity, and experiences of others in a productive way. This is the essence of empathy and most women are naturals at it, having been socialized from early childhood to be so. We tend to care about people and their well-being. We want to respect and protect their emotions. Naturally inquisitive, we can engage in an empathic conversation just minutes after meeting someone for the first time. I am no exception. My husband says that I will talk to a stop sign. I tend to be attuned to people's emotional states. I often find myself trying to rescue others from embarrassment, undue criticism, or sticky social situations.

When I interviewed Michelle Riddell, vice-president of digital communication at the Educational Media Foundation (owner of the popular K-LOVE Radio Network and Air 1 Radio Network in Southern California), she related the following story of empathy:

> I am so intrigued about actively listening and learning whom I'm speaking to. I talk about myself very little during the conversation because, in my mind, I feel it makes me a better leader when I know who I'm about to serve and what they need from me. At an employee banquet several years ago, after everybody had already been seated and the lights had been dimmed, I spotted a couple near the entrance, obviously late. I imagined the difficulty they would have in finding their seats in the darkened room with so many people already seated

in a maze of round tables. I got up from my seat, went, and escorted "Amy" and her husband to open seats. Why did I do that? Because it was the right thing to do. My VP status didn't matter. What mattered was empathizing with an employee who was in an awkward situation. Amy remembered and expressed her gratitude to me for that kindness over the following years.

Leading like a woman allows us to maintain the behaviors we are already comfortable with, which include the following:

- demonstrating compassion when others experience a personal loss or crisis
- being interested in the personal lives of subordinates (birthdays, anniversaries, etc.)
- showing support for the ambitions and desired career path of others

As women lead alongside men and model how to be emotionally savvy, we can expect to see higher employee morale, increased productivity, and more company loyalty.

3

NURTURING:
Finding and Mining the Gold in Others

You don't build a business, you build people,
then people build the business.

—Zig Ziglar, American author and motivational speaker

What image comes to your mind when you hear the word *nurturing*? A woman nursing a baby? Feeding a puppy? Growing a plant? The concept of nurturing has gotten a misleading reputation because it's been used most often to describe the soft, passive caring, or coddling, of somebody or some organism—usually by a female. Honestly, when was the last time that you heard someone describe a male authority figure as being nurturing? Perhaps this is why some women leaders who want a reputation for being tough avoid behaving in any way associated with such delicate behavior. Notwithstanding, numerous studies show that women, except for those who insist on leading like a man, have a stronger propensity to encourage or nurture subordinate development. I interviewed several ladies who modeled this truth.

Dr. Beverly Crawford (aka "Dr. Bam") served on the staff of one of the fastest-growing ministries in the United States for several years before answering God's call to establish Bible Enrichment Fellowship International Church in Inglewood, California. She grew up as a homeless youth in South Central Los Angeles. Her experience led her to empower women around the world through powerful teaching, mentoring, and special programs. Dr. Bam is also a pioneer in the male-dominated field of pastoral ministry. Her direct communication style and nurturing leadership style seem to be studies in contrasts. Here is how she explained it during our interview.

Me: Dr. Bam, you are a female pastor with a significant number of men—strong men—in your congregation. What do you think attracts them to your leadership, and how do you nurture them?

Dr. Bam: When I started the ministry, my elders were former marines, police officers, and other high-ranking police personnel. These men knew how to respect authority and what it meant to follow directives. They proved to be powerful role models for a lot of the men serving today. But beyond that, I do have a strong personality, and I've learned to just be myself with them. I don't talk down to them. I am very mindful of how I'd make a request of them or how I correct them. Even when I must correct, I don't sugarcoat the issue. I think they like that. Also, I have the spiritual sensitivity to know when they're hurting. That's when I pour in the oil and the wine of compassion so that their wounds can heal.

When Dr. Bam launched the ministry, she endured persecution from religious leaders who felt that the Bible forbade her to assume the role of a pastor. Undeterred, she forged ahead and maintained her unique and inspiring style of being a strong, nurturing leader.

Popular Hollywood filmmaker Ava DuVernay models a similar style and embraces it with pride.

Me: Ava, what traditionally feminine trait has served you best in your leadership role?

Ava: I think there's a maternal quality that I bring to the director's role on a set that many male directors just don't have because it's not a part of them. You know as women, most of us want to make sure that people are okay. There was a time earlier in my career as a publicist when I would go on sets with male directors. The people would be busily doing their work, but they didn't look like they were enjoying each other. I like to welcome people to the set with a smile and a hug. I like to talk to folks, to get to know people a little more personally. I think that's definitely a feminine quality that I don't shy away from.

According to an article by Gabrielle Anagnostopoulos, co-chair of the popular Queens Commerce Leadership Summit, "one member of Ava's crew described her influence on set as something he has never seen before. He marveled at the way she harnessed the collective vision, drive, and belief of her team to foster the development of rare fellowships that are difficult to find."[1]

Dr. Bam and Ava continue to create environments that cause their teams to be fully engaged and enjoy a sense of belonging and connection to a cause higher than the work itself. That is a critical component of organizational success and is usually attributed to the presence of a woman.

Nurturing Poor Performers

I terminated quite a few people during my corporate career. During my first decade or so as a manager, I had no tolerance for underperformers. Those were the days when I mistakenly thought I had to lead like a man and to employ a no-nonsense style in order to be respected. Further, with all the stress of meeting various deadlines, controlling budgets, and other challenges common to the financial management and reporting function, I felt that I didn't have time to invest in the development of employees who did not appear to be proactive in pursuing their own growth. I thought, "Whatever happened to initiative?" I wanted everyone I hired to "hit the ground running"—just as they had implied they could do during the interview.

Of course, I didn't hesitate to provide honest feedback on their performance, but I'm sure it was not constructive as it was accompanied by body language that showed my disappointment and frustration. While I was quick to point out their specific shortcomings, I rarely developed strategies to help them overcome them. It was after I attended a mandatory management class on employee development that I learned that one of my key roles as a leader was to help employees reach their maximum potential. By criticizing them and hoping they would quit before I fired them, I'm sure I created a high level of job insecurity as well as a vicious cycle of underperformance. I developed a new mind-set after the class and committed to grooming those who had potential—even when it had to be discovered.

There was "Carl," who was so determined to always have an answer to every question I asked that he would blurt out the first thing that came to mind. Many times, his responses had absolutely no relevance to my question. I suppose his anxiety had kept him from hearing it! One day I asked him, "What happened in your childhood experience to cause you to resort to this type of behavior?" He explained, almost to the point of tears, that he'd been raised by a very critical and impatient father who never validated him nor encouraged him in his pursuits—and always demanded an answer to his questions. I assured Carl that it was okay to say "I don't know" or "Let me get back to you on that." My decision to nurture him to excellence resulted in a long-term, loyal, and supportive employee.

Nurturing through affirmation and encouragement is crucial but it is equally important to engage another level of nurturing: pruning. Many years ago, not knowing a lot about gardening, I wanted to understand our gardener's intentions when he suggested that we have several of the trees around our house pruned. It was a pricey proposition compared to the regular gardening work. I researched several sources and learned that pruning is the process of selectively removing unwanted branches from a tree to improve its structure and to direct new, healthy growth. One gardening expert explained, "A proper prune is both an investment in the long-term health of your plants and in the overall look and safety of your property."[2] I experienced an a-ha moment when I realized that employees or volunteers often need to be gently shaped or pruned to maximize their potential. I finally decided to stop *uprooting* and discarding them and to start helping them self-prune. I learned to be very specific about their unproductive behavior and gently guide them to disconnect from it. Yes, it took more time to correct the unwanted tendencies, but the benefits ultimately outweighed the cost.

Nurturing Superstars

Most organizations have employees who excel above all others in their creativity, productivity, initiative, or other areas. They are a godsend and the company's biggest asset. Nurturing these superstars involves a lot more than a few "atta-boys" or "atta-girls" for a job well done. A good leader must determine what it takes to motivate and retain such employees. All superstars are not motivated equally. You will need to be proactive in finding out what's on employees' wish lists for work. Be willing to consider flex time, improved working environment conditions, and other motivating benefits. Stay competitive by being in the know about what similar organizations are providing.

While a paycheck is not the only motivator, good compensation is a fine place to start. I've seen several organizations take complete advantage of key employees—especially females—because they never requested raises or promotions. When the employee wised up and realized how valuable they were, they moved to greener pastures, leaving a gaping hole in the organization's knowledge base.

After finding out what motivates your key performers and what challenges they would like to pursue, consider the following winning strategies:

- When assigning tasks or projects, give your top performers a wide berth of freedom within a framework. Micromanaging is demotivating to creative, self-sufficient employees. Of course, as the leader, you will establish the "what" or goal for a project, but trust them to decide the "how," or the best approach for a successful outcome. This is not to say that you should be totally hands-off, but it will demonstrate your confidence in their ability to be creative when you only require periodic reporting. Plus, it gives them an opportunity to shine.

- Don't assume that superstars don't need to be encouraged or acknowledged for their performance just because they and everybody else know they do superior work. Every person wants to be appreciated. Everyone. Therefore, always acknowledge everyone's contributions lest you run the risk of alienating the rest of your team and causing them to resent you and the superstars.

- Be sure to keep the workload balanced between the superstars and the other staff. The fact that an employee "can" perform several key functions is no reason to overload them with excessive assignments. Beware of burning them out. Monitor what's on their plates and consider reassigning their existing tasks before adding more responsibilities.

- Don't hold the superstars back. When I worked in a certain company, my superiors habitually conscripted my administrative assistants. The word was out that if someone had worked for me, they had developed a broad spectrum of practical skills and social and relational know-how. I can't say that I joyfully released them, but I never held anyone back. If your employee would be suited for a growth opportunity, encourage them to pursue it. Don't have a scarcity mentality; if God provided once, he can do it again. Even within your department, look for ways to give employees increasing responsibility and relieve them of tasks they have mastered.

> When assigning tasks or projects, give
> your top performers a wide berth of
> freedom within a framework.

Nurturing Versus Mothering

During a stint at a certain organization, I often found myself mothering my subordinates who were experiencing troubling domestic issues. I also tended to administer "corporate spankings" if their personal problems persisted and affected their ability to perform their responsibilities. This was the case with "Dorothy," one of our accounting clerks. She was a single parent whose boyfriend often physically abused her. Since I too had come from a home fraught with domestic violence, I showed empathy toward her situation. As the organization's chief financial officer, I ran a department that was responsible for preparing timely financial statements and analysis for internal and external users. When Dorothy began to miss too many days or when she got behind in her assignments, I took her to task. She became very demoralized and exclaimed, "I thought you were my friend!" Obviously, she was frustrated by what she perceived as my mixed signals. She had assumed that my empathy afforded her a privileged status. I did indeed care about her personal well-being; however, my primary responsibility was to my employer. I found myself caught between showing compassion and commanding results. To boot, there was a culture of "mercy" throughout the organization and firings were rare. Obviously, I had mismanaged my innate tendency to nurture and had failed to clearly communicate my expectations and the consequences of not meeting them. Dorothy and I had a heart-to-heart discussion. I assured her that while I valued her as part of the team, she would need to take steps to resolve her personal issues so that her job would not be jeopardized. I also resolved inwardly to use more wisdom going forward in determining the extent of my nurturing.

Showing compassion to employees is one of the traits women bring to the table in a way that engenders employee loyalty and a sense of belonging. Employees tend to be much more engaged in the organization's goals and objectives. They own them and speak in terms of "we" versus "they" when discussing company projects and goals: "We are building a new facility." "Our systems are the best."

How Much Nurturing?

As you rise through the ranks or become more influential, more women (and men) will desire to know the secrets of your success. Since the subject of women's empowerment will be a hotbed issue for years to come, you must be careful to manage expectations regarding how much time to invest in nurturing the careers of other women (or other people of your ethnicity). Don't let the guilt of not being able to fulfill requests to be a personal mentor cause you to take on an unfair burden within and outside your organization. Decide now to prioritize such efforts considering your family and other priorities. One practical suggestion is to be proactive in making your wisdom available in a digital format such as "My Top 10 Rules for Success," "10 Mistakes to Avoid on the Way to the Top," or a short YouTube video that captures your philosophy on your professional life. These quick tools go a long way in saying to others, "I can't commit time to you, but here are some lessons I've learned that may help you in your journey."

Nurturing employees is all about creating an environment and culture within your sphere of influence that gives them space and opportunity to grow and achieve their highest potential. We can boldly bring our natural affinity for nurturing to the table knowing that like all our inherent traits, it must be managed to be effective.

COMMUNICATIVE:
Connecting Effectively

When ideas are communicated effectively,
people follow and change.

—Nancy Duarte, American author and speaker

They did not run out of manpower, materials, or money. Their unity was so remarkable that it impressed God. But the builders of the Tower of Babel were forced to halt construction of the infamous skyscraper due to the lack of one deal-breaking factor: the ability to communicate. After the great flood of Noah's day, God ordered the survivors to scatter across the earth and repopulate it. But they had different plans. They decided to settle down in one place and to build a tower that reached into the heavens—making a name for themselves. Because the project was being done in complete disobedience to God's command, he confused their language and they had to abandon their efforts.[1] Lesson learned: If you can't communicate, you can't build anything—a marriage, an organization, a team.

Good leadership and good communication go hand in hand. Fortunately, this is an inherent trait in women leaders. Being communicative is being forthcoming in sharing or exchanging information via oral or written means. "Leadership communication is defined as inspiring and encouraging an individual or a group by systematic and meaningful sharing of information by using excellent communication skills."[2] Communicating requires one to be skilled enough to clearly express ideas and information with a variety of people including superiors, subordinates, customers, or one's peers.

One of the most critical elements of being communicative is authenticity. It's important to just be yourself. When you interact with others, avoid using corporate-speak or impressive multisyllable words that they may not understand. Who you are and what you value should shine through every time you speak. Susan Tardanico, founder and CEO of the Authentic Leadership Alliance, says, "People want real. People respect real. People follow real. Don't disguise who you are. People will never willingly follow a phony."[3]

One of the most critical elements of being
communicative is authenticity.
It's important to just be yourself.

Another factor in being communicative is being visible. In order to communicate well, you can't always be out of sight. Don't hide behind emails, notes, or instant messages. Show up in person as often as you can. Allow people to get to know you on a deeper, below-the-surface level. You will find them more responsive to your plans and requests when they can connect them to a human being.

We often think of communicating as only speaking; however, listening is a vital part of the process. When you are a good listener, others learn to trust and respect you, for only by listening can you gain an understanding of someone else's perspective.

Tips for Being a More Effective Communicator

Even though women are wired to be master communicators, we should never stop sharpening our skills so that the message we send is the exact message that is received. Try these tips to take your communication to the next level:

- *Be direct and simple.* Gracefully say what you mean and mean what you say. Don't hide behind vague or complicated words. Simplify your message so that anyone who listens can easily grasp it. The apostle Paul was a highly educated man, but he wisely refrained from preaching above the heads of his audience. "My message and my preaching were very plain. Rather than using clever and persuasive speeches, I relied only on the power of the Holy Spirit. I did this so you would trust not in human wisdom but in the power of God."[4]

- *Communicate frequently.* Communicate as often as you can and through as many different mediums as you can, including remote video and so on. People often learn and consume information in different ways, so it's a good idea to give them options.

- *Encourage feedback.* Always be willing to hear another perspective. When you give a directive or offer an idea, pause and allow the other person to respond. Many leaders are not always open to input. Don't be that person. Remember the 80/20 rule: Listen 80 percent of the time and speak 20 percent of the time.

- *Walk your talk.* Don't be a hypocrite. If your words and actions are inconsistent, you will lose credibility. Always remember that even when you are not speaking, you are communicating. Nothing will cause people to mistrust you more than not being a person of your word or displaying a lack of integrity in some way.

- *Be a storyteller.* Stories serve as great visual illustrations. They breathe life into your goals or vision. Thus learning how to be a good storyteller will enhance your communication. It helps others vividly grasp the message. Jesus knew the power of a story. "Jesus used many similar stories and illustrations to teach the people as much as they could understand. In fact, in his public ministry he never taught without using parables."[5] Stories are memorable and repeatable and more likely to be shared with others.

Benefits of Being an Effective Communicator

If you run an organization, you will experience greater loyalty, stability, and buy-in to the company's goals if you are a good communicator. Employee morale significantly improves when employees and team members feel communication freely flows both ways. Effective communication has the power to engender loyalty in those you serve. I ran into a former coworker a few years after I'd moved on from a former employer. She immediately lamented, "We really miss you. We are kept in the dark; everything is a secret now." I made it a point to teach the members of the finance team how to read and interpret the monthly financial statements and to show them how their function helped develop them. They were able to transfer much of the knowledge into a better understanding of their own financial status.

Another benefit of being communicative is that it minimizes misunderstandings. Clear and frequent communication keeps others in the loop on changes or new developments.

Male Versus Female Leaders: Communication Strengths and Weaknesses

It's no secret that men and women communicate differently, but what does this mean for leadership roles? Carol Kinsey Goman, PhD, conducted a study and found obvious strengths and weaknesses in the communication styles of both men and women. Women's top communication strengths were the ability to pick up nonverbal cues, good listening skills, and the ability to display empathy. Men's top communication strengths were physical presence, to-the-point interactions, and body language that signals power.

Women's top communication weaknesses were being overly emotional, failing to get to the point, and not appearing authoritative.

Men's top communication weaknesses were being overly blunt and direct, being insensitive, and being too confident in their opinion. Dr. Goman says there is no best communication style for workplace interactions. The skills of both women and men can come in handy based on the situation in which they find themselves. For example, "women may have the edge in collaborative environments (where listening skills, inclusive body language, and empathy are more highly valued), and men are usually believed to 'take charge' more readily." Thus, they are "viewed as more effective in environments where decisiveness is critical."[6]

Overcommunicating

While good communication is important, it is equally crucial to avoid being an oversharer. Don't be a Chatty Cathy and divulge more information than necessary. Some people can only handle so much. Your extra information may cause them anxiety. When communicating, ask yourself, "Does this person *want* or *need* to know this?" Also, in an attempt to be more relatable, female leaders may be tempted to share more details of their personal lives than necessary. You must walk a fine line between openness and too much information. "Great communicators say what needs to be said, when it needs to be said and to whom it needs to be said—nothing more, nothing less."[7]

"Effective communication can boost customer satisfaction, improve work performance and result in stronger partnerships."[8] Consider these stats:

- One in four employees surveyed has quit, or knows someone who has quit, due to a lack of transparency and communication in the workplace.

- Only 10 percent of employees surveyed were aware of their company's progress in real time.

- More than four out of five employees surveyed wanted to hear more frequently from their bosses about how their company was doing.

- More than 90 percent of employees surveyed said they would rather hear bad news than no news.[9]

How do you stack up against these stats? Is it time to survey your employees or followers to determine if you are communicating effectively and frequently enough for the dynamics of your organization? Regardless of your role as a female leader—whether you lead a team, run a company, are an author or influencer, or are an entrepreneur—communication skills are vital to your success.

INTUITIVE:
Going with Your Gut

*Who gives intuition to the heart
and instinct to the mind?*

Job 38:36 NLT

I had taken the aerospace budget director's job as a last resort. The venture capital firm where I had worked as a vice president for the past ten years was being shuttered and I needed employment. The job was going to be a challenge because I didn't know the industry nor their lingo. Everyone spoke in acronyms and sounded like they were from another planet. It required years of on-the-job experience before one really became familiar with them. I was scared to death.

It was no secret that I was an affirmative action hire. The company had a notorious record of blatant racism, but the government was cracking down by requiring more minorities in high visibility positions before granting the lucrative, multimillion-dollar contracts. Adding to my fear was the fact that they had given me a 20 percent raise over my former position. What if I couldn't perform? It wouldn't just be that "Deborah Smith Pegues" failed; I carried the burden of my entire race. By the grace of God, nobody was going to say this African American was inadequate. Notwithstanding, being a CPA with an MBA in business finance put my credentials a bit higher than most of the executives in the department where I would be working. Still, I lacked industry experience. It was going to be a "tough row to hoe," and the company knew it. Therefore, management assigned a mentor to help minimize my learning curve. I could tell that she hated the assignment—and for good reason. I was paid a higher salary than she because of my advanced degree. Personally, I believe experience should always trump education, but I don't make the rules—which is why I chose to go to graduate school. My "mentor" did as little mentoring as possible. But God was with me. For example, I would often feel a strong urge to prepare a special report or financial analysis. When it was completed, within hours or just a day or so at most, someone from the executive team would ask if my department could produce such a report. I'd whip it out, making every effort to hide my satisfaction at being ahead of the game.

Once, the top brass called the finance executives in on a Saturday morning leading up to an upcoming overhead rate negotiation with the government. It appeared from my team's forecast of revenues and operating costs that the rate was going to be at a historic high. As we sat around the big oval conference table, different executives expressed that the rate would probably not come in as high as my department had forecasted. I didn't have enough experience on the job to argue my point adamantly, but I felt a strong urge to stick with our forecast. My fellow workers, including my boss, doubted my projection. I held my ground. Several months later, the rate we had forecast proved to be accurate. During the next quarter's review of the overhead rates, I felt joyously vindicated when the chief financial officer proclaimed, "There is no one who can forecast these rates like Deborah Pegues." Some may call it intuition, but I knew it was the sheer grace of God that had revealed that information with such accuracy.

What Is Intuition?

Intuition is possessing the ability to perceive the character or motivations of another, to have insight into the reality or outcome of a situation without the benefit of foreknowledge. We've all experienced that moment in time when we were certain of something that we could not logically be sure of. We just "had a feeling" that something was not right or that something was going to happen. That's intuition—a gut feeling when "something" inside puts you on alert. Women are generally known to be more intuitive than men. There are significant differences in the structure of the male and female brain. The female brain structure may give women the advantage as it has more developed areas that enhance speech and verbal processing. Intuition has increasingly gained more respect over the years. Men have intuition as well, but theirs is not as highly developed as it is in women according to scientific studies.

Intuition and discernment often work hand in hand, but they are not the same. While intuition refers to a gut feeling or a hunch, discernment helps you wisely recognize and use your intuition when you need it. When looked at this way, we see that intuition isn't just a reliance on flighty emotions but is grounded in intelligence. Intuition can cause unnecessary fear or worry, and discernment can help you reel in those emotions and not let them incapacitate you.

According to *Forbes*, intuition is essential in leadership. In their book *The Feminine Revolution*, Amy Stanton and Catherine Connors discuss the fact that in today's workplace, flexibility and versatility are more important than ever, which means female leaders are essential. "As founders and business leaders, we have this wonderful opportunity to create workplace cultures that encourage intuition."[1]

While intuition refers to a gut feeling or a hunch,
discernment helps you wisely recognize
and use your intuition when you need it.

How to Develop Your Intuition

- *Recognize it.* Be on alert to recognize when you are having an intuitive moment. If you find yourself thinking about someone more than usual, and they call you up shortly thereafter, know that it was likely your intuition at work.

- *Silence your inner critic.* Many times, we try to rationalize away our intuitive thoughts, thinking we should be more logical and rely on facts. The next time you have an intuition about something, don't analyze it or argue with yourself about it. Give in to it and see what happens. Realizing you were correct will enable you to have more faith in the process the next time.

- *Embrace your creativity.* Creative activities such as painting, drawing, writing, and crafts allow your mind to flow freely. They can put you in a mindset that allows you to be more open to new ideas and insights.

- *Take notes.* Carry a small journal or notebook (or use your electronic notes on your cell phone) to record your thoughts, gut feelings, and hunches. Sometimes, we have such reactions throughout the day, but then we forget about them. Writing them down will allow you to review them at your leisure and remember fleeting, but important, feelings that occurred throughout the day.

- *Get physical.* Go for a walk or a run or even take a shower. Often, taking a break from the daily grind frees our minds to mull over problems and come up with solutions.

- *Evaluate your dreams.* Often our dreams are windows into our subconscious. Dreams help us process information and deal with stress or unacknowledged desires. They can reveal deep and symbolic messages that escape our attention when we are awake.

　　I once had a dream where a woman's name was spelled out in huge box-car letters on a blank canvas. When I awakened, I Googled the name, and finally located her at her place of employment in the Midwest. I had a hard time convincing her that I wasn't a crank but had "met" her through a dream. After several conversations, her getting familiar with my background and an acknowledgment that we both listened to some of the same spiritual leaders, we became phone friends. I prayed her through some tough times, and we ultimately met and had dinner together in Los Angeles. I still marvel at this whole thing.

- *Wrestle with the problem before bed.* Popular advice says we should try to clear our minds so that we can peacefully go to sleep. However, if you are wrestling with a problem, thinking about it and its possible solutions before bed can prepare your mind to process the problem while you're asleep. When you wake up in the morning, you might find that you have come up with the solution.

- *Evaluate the past.* There have, no doubt, been many times in the past where you had an intuition and didn't act on it. You kicked yourself for not listening to yourself. Recall those times and allow them to bolster your confidence in the future.

- *Take a drive.* Like being creative or going for a run, taking a drive to nowhere in particular can be a relaxing activity that frees your mind and allows your subconscious to take over.

- *Pray.* Most important of all, when we need to make a decision, we often have a choice we are leaning toward. However, we second-guess ourselves by going back and forth, unable to decide. In responding to Job, the suffering patriarch, God declares, through a rhetorical question, that he is the source of intuition. "Who gives intuition to the heart and instinct to the mind?"[2] So don't dismiss the concept of intuition as something mystical or magical. It is God-given. Simply ask the Holy Spirit to lead you as to when to rely on it.

When to Rely on Intuition

While intuition is helpful in many situations, there is a time to use it and a time not to use it. A good time to use intuition is when you already have expertise in an area. For example, we often rely on intuition when driving. On the other hand, if we are learning how to mountain climb, we would rely less on intuition. We would need more than a hunch or a gut feeling to determine whether a mountain path is safe. According to the *Harvard Business Review*, it takes about ten years to develop the expertise needed for accurate, intuitive judgments. Expertise in an area provides essential repetition and feedback, which aids in helping us determine whether our decisions were good ones and where we need to make changes.

Another time to go with your gut feeling is when you face a problem where there isn't enough data to make an objective decision.

The amount of time you have available to make a decision should also determine whether or not you use intuition. Of course, in such a situation, you still need to use discernment and to evaluate all the information you have available. The important thing to remember is that even when intuition is relied upon, it is still backed by data in your subconscious. It's not blindly following feelings or baseless emotions.

Neuroscience has increasingly demonstrated that intuition can be just as logical as hard facts. It is merely the assimilation of all the facts and life experiences we have stored in the recesses of our minds coming to the forefront when we need them. The brain is constantly working to make connections that may not be obvious at first but are nonetheless real. Dr. John Townsend, author of *Leadership Beyond Reason*, explains, "You ignore what is beyond reason to your peril...Leaders who don't pay attention to the subjective will miss a great deal of importance."[3] Once you begin to trust your intuition more, you can allow it to make a positive impact on important decisions.

Christians should be cautioned that not all our inner thoughts and feelings should be heeded, for they can lead us astray. "There is a path before each person that seems right, but it ends in death."[4] That "feeling" or "something" must be submitted to the Holy Spirit's discernment for our next step. He is the fountain of wisdom and understanding that Jesus sent specifically to teach and guide us.

MOTIVATIONAL:
Inspiring Results

*If the first woman God ever made was strong
enough to turn the world upside down all
alone, these together ought to be able to turn
it back and get it right side up again.*

—Sojourner Truth, American abolitionist

Although you may have heard more stories about women's ability to manipulate than to motivate, women leaders have an advantage over their male peers when it comes to motivating employees. A Gallup study, *State of the American Manager: Analytics and Advice for Leaders*, found that 33 percent of employees are engaged when a woman runs the show, compared to 25 percent with a man at the helm. Female managers also tend to be more enthusiastic about their own jobs than their male counterparts. Gallup found 41 percent of female managers feel engaged at work compared to 35 percent of male managers.[1]

As a leader, motivation should always be your priority. Motivated team members don't just show up to do a job. They take great joy in what they do and will go above and beyond what the situation calls for. Motivation always offers a win-win situation for both the leader and the team member. Great leaders know how to rally their team around shared values and clarity of purpose. For team members to be motivated, they must believe their efforts will lead to specific outcomes, and these outcomes must be subjectively important to them.

**For team members to be motivated,
they must believe their efforts will lead to specific
outcomes, and these outcomes must
be subjectively important to them.**

The Five Categories of Workers

Psychological researcher Ilona Jerabek says team members can be divided into five clusters, based on how they prefer to be motivated:[2]

- *Trailblazers* want to significantly impact others and leave their mark on the world. They are very social and are motivated by the desire to satisfy, identity and purpose, learning, creativity, and fun and enjoyment.

- *Workhorses* enjoy structure and want to do their job well. You can rely on them to show up on time and give you their best work. They are motivated by achievement, stability, financial reward, structure and order, recognition and appreciation, power, and status.

- *Heavyweights* thrive in a fast-paced, high-pressure environment. They are interested in influencing others and high achievement. They are often workaholics and enjoy challenges and obstacles. Their top motivators are achievement, responsibility, active/high-pressure work environment, power, status, and contribution/legacy.

- *Gen-Yers* (aka "millennials"; born between 1980 and 1994) are a challenge to most leaders who view them as unmotivated, spoiled brats who expect promotions without paying their dues. However, they simply want to love the work they do. They aren't afraid of hard work and thrive in team-oriented environments that encourage enthusiasm and an open mind. They love to think outside the box. They are motivated by inspiration, social contact, financial reward, recognition and appreciation, creativity, power, status, mobility, contribution/legacy, and fun and enjoyment.

- *Explorers* prefer variety over routine; therefore, they often don't stay in jobs for the long term. They enjoy learning new things and are very creative. They are motivated by learning, change, variety, job-hopping, creativity, independence, power, mobility, and contribution/legacy.

Based on this information, leaders should attempt to find out what category their team members fall into and respond accordingly. Doing so allows you to determine what motivates your team members and enables you to create fulfilling roles and jobs for them.

Understanding What Motivates Others

Motivation requires a basic understanding of human behavior. When team members feel positive emotions, they are more likely to be internally motivated. Therefore, it is important for leaders to understand what inspires loyalty and enthusiasm. Here are some ways you can create an atmosphere conducive to motivation:

1. *Figure out what motivates your team:* What are their interests, goals, and aspirations? What are they passionate about? It is important to really get to know your team members; otherwise, you have no hope of truly motivating them. This is called emotional engagement. My interview with Barry E. Knight—CEO of BEK Impact Company, a popular leadership coaching firm, and author of *Impactability*—bears out this truth:

   Me: Barry, based on your corporate and ministry coaching experience, what area of leadership development do you feel women need to make a priority?

Barry: The first thought that comes to mind is that a woman must be capable of motivating and inspiring her team. People cannot resist being inspired. If I were coaching a female leader or CEO, I would tell her to sit down with each member of her team individually and find out what I call their "motivational hack." Ask, "What is it that drives or motivates you and keeps you on track?" Everyone is motivated differently; they are not all inspired by the same carrot.

I worked for a female manager once who came in like blockbusters, making changes immediately. It backfired on her. She did not get the team's support. She could have taken a different approach. She could have said to me, "Barry, you've been working here two years. Tell me what I don't know about the office." She would have garnered so much more respect from us. I think she put too much focus on trying to prove that she was tough—even though she was female. Her actions were very demotivating.

2. *Provide purposeful work.* In his book *Give and Take*, Professor Adam Grant says that "when people know how their work makes a difference, they feel energized to contribute more."[3] He says one way to do this is to have people meet those they serve, if possible. Seeing the impact of one's work serves as a powerful motivator.

3. *Give them what they need.* There is nothing worse than being assigned a task and not having everything you need to efficiently do the job. Ask team members what they need to do their job better. Almost everyone will have one or more suggestions, and when they tell you, act on what you learn if it is within your power to do so.

4. *Implement one-on-one conversations.* Get to know the members of your team so you can strengthen your relationship

on an individual level. Listen to their problems and suggestions without judgment and discuss any performance issues. Give praise where it is due.

5. *Trust them.* Team members can tell when their leaders do not trust them. Even if the mistrust is unspoken, it can be felt. Don't be afraid to trust your team with increasing responsibility. Give them an assignment and allow them to handle it. You hired them for their particular skill set, so trust that you made the right decision.

6. *Be liberal with praise.* Some leaders think it's wise to withhold praise to motivate team members in their work. However, "individuals who receive regular recognition and praise…increase their individual productivity [and] increase engagement among their colleagues."[4]

7. *Encourage them to develop new skills.* This goes beyond giving team members another computer or sending them to a training class. Tap into their natural strengths and inclinations and help them develop for future roles and responsibilities. If you do this, they will be less likely to grow discontent or desire to move to a different organization.

Motivation Versus Manipulation

It is important for female leaders to understand the essence of motivation and not to confuse it with manipulation. Motivation refers to having the ability to inspire or influence others to act by modeling, urging, advising, or appealing to their reason and core needs. Motivation is a crucial leadership skill, as it translates employees' knowledge, skills, and abilities into effort and performance by determining the direction, intensity, and duration of work-related behaviors. The key point to remember regarding motivation is that it is about the other party's self-interest. In other words, it is hard to motivate someone if they don't already see the benefit to themselves.

Their goal is to improve their life in some way, and you are motivating them to do that.

On the other hand, manipulation refers to instilling fear in someone to cause them to do what you want, often using some sort of deceit in the process. Rather than appealing to one's self-interest, those who manipulate are concerned about their own self-preservation. Manipulation is selfish, while motivation is selfless. Manipulation as a strategy may work in the short term, but it is ineffective in the long term. Manipulation has no place as a leadership strategy.

The following chart compares the differences between motivation and manipulation:[5]

MOTIVATION	MANIPULATION
Cares about the person and the task	Cares only about the task at hand
Empowers the team	Controls the team
Fosters loyalty	Fosters resentment
Driven by love	Driven by pride
Values the team	Devalues the team
Grounded in substance	Grounded in style
Uses positive adjectives	Uses negative adjectives
Is supportive	Is critical
Asks what team members want	Determines what team members need
Breeds trust	Breeds fear and distrust
Offers alternatives	Offers absolutes
Attempts to positively influence	Attempts to deceive

There are substantial differences in what motivates women as opposed to men. For example, it would seem logical that everyone is motivated by money, but money is the fifth most important motivator for men, whereas it is twelfth for women. Researcher Ilona Jerabek has found that motivation is multidimensional and identified the top ten motivators as follows: "achievement; learning; inspiration (the chance to inspire others); creativity; fun and enjoyment; improvement; financial reward; change and variety; identity and purpose; and stability."[6]

Organizations and companies have traditionally tried to provide incentives for their workers to perform in ways that benefit their bottom line. While this may have worked years ago, this technique has fallen out of favor, which is why many people are unhappy in their work. Learning to inspire and motivate people, though it may take more time, is a necessary skill. While it may be easier to bark orders and rule people with fear, it is not effective in the long run—especially coming from a woman.

Good leaders communicate openly and don't rely on manipulation tactics to get tasks accomplished. They are approachable and open to new ideas. They give praise freely when it is deserved, understanding that criticism is usually a demotivator. When we acknowledge people's efforts, they feel more confident, which encourages them to do an even better job next time. This is the power of motivation.

In his book *1,001 Ways to Reward Employees*, author Bob Nelson claims that "the top two drivers of employee performance are being able to say, 'I am able to make a difference at work' and 'I have been recognized recently for what I do.'" He states that more than 68 percent of those he interviewed had never even been told "thank you."[7] Women are more likely to show praise and appreciation than their male counterparts.

Ultimately, the leader herself can serve as a powerful source of motivation. Team members are motivated by those who walk the walk and talk the talk. The best leaders serve as role models who embody the values and work ethics they ask their team members to emulate. When you personally demonstrate what you want for your team, there is a better chance that they will follow your lead.

RESILIENT/PERSISTENT:
Bouncing Back and Moving Forward

Tough times never last, but tough people do.
—Robert H. Schuller, host of *The Hour of Power* (1970–2010)

At age 11, Cheryl Prewitt was in a horrible automobile accident that left her with a scarred face, a body cast, and a wheelchair as her means of mobility. Coupled with a life of poverty and sexual abuse, her future looked bleak. Despite the odds, she entered and lost pageants for five years before winning the title of Miss America 1980. Winning the pageant was a springboard for Cheryl to launch her ministry of preaching the gospel of Jesus Christ as she was invited into churches, schools, women's retreats, and television appearances. She married Harry Salem II in 1985, and they formed Salem Family Ministries. Her heart was broken in 1999 when her six-year-old daughter Gabrielle passed away after being diagnosed with a brain tumor. Cheryl redirected her pain into her passion for the lost and hurting. Her books and CDs have brought hope through her ministry in prisons, women's shelters, inner-city outreaches, disaster relief programs, and other platforms. Cheryl Prewitt Salem's name has become synonymous with resilience and persistence.

Resilience Versus Persistence

Resilience and persistence often work hand and hand. While resilience refers to bouncing back after enduring a crisis, persistence refers to the ability to steadfastly pursue an objective despite opposition, delays, or other disadvantages. Both resilience and persistence are important because one must not only recover from a setback but have the endurance to continue and not give up.

Persistence naturally requires being resilient, as you can't persist if you never get back up. On the other hand, it is important not to take persistence to the extreme. It may seem reasonable to keep going when the odds are stacked against us, but there are times when we just need to learn to let go.

Resilience is an important character trait, and it is in our DNA as women. Women are accustomed to continually resisting the odds as we find ourselves often pushed aside when it comes to professional advancement. We quickly learn that we must reframe the challenges of gender inequality and face them as opportunities to become stronger.

Characteristics of resilience include the following:

- continuing to be productive while persevering

- having a determined spirit

- celebrating small wins

- having a persistent mind-set

- exhibiting a "can-do" attitude

- doing your best when things are at their worst

- accepting circumstances outside of your control

- exhibiting problem-solving skills

- learning and growing from past challenges and mistakes

- not being afraid to ask for help

- embracing opportunities for change

- adapting to correction and circumstances

Maya Angelou: A Resilient Female Leader

The list of female leaders who have faced adversity or difficulty and have risen above the challenges is extensive. Many revolutionized their industries and environments and influenced attitudes around the world.

Famed poetess and activist Maya Angelou was one such woman. She said, "You may not control all the events that happen to you, but you can decide not to be reduced by them."[1] And she was certainly a living witness of that statement. She was sexually abused by her mother's boyfriend at a young age, and after her abuser was found dead, she blamed herself for disclosing the assault. Believing her voice had killed him, she was mute for five years. But in her silence, she developed a love for books, which would greatly affect her future. Later in life, she worked as a prostitute and a madam. Maya rose above her early struggles and became a household name, with writings that span several decades in her seven autobiographies. Her career included public speaking; writing books, poems, and screenplays; and directing and acting. She received countless awards, including the Presidential Medal of Freedom and the National Medal of Arts. She was nominated for the Pulitzer Prize and a Tony Award and won several Grammy Awards. Maya Angelou rose above the tragedies and troubles of her youth to become a woman who was well-admired and respected worldwide.

Strategies for Handling Adversity

When adversity rears its head, it is wise to follow some predetermined guidelines as to how you will cope. Here are some strategies that have helped me to overcome many problems.

- *Maintain a good attitude.* I have a trio of truths that I hold fast to when problems arise. I label them the "I.R.S." of adversity:

    (1) *Trouble is inevitable.* "Man who is born of woman is of few days and full of trouble."[2] No one is going to

escape the physical, emotional, relational, or financial pains, losses, frustrations, inequities, and inconveniences of living on planet Earth. Everyone reading this right now is either experiencing a trial, has just come through a time of testing, or will face a problem in the future. This is not the time to bemoan this reality or to be anxious about what lies ahead. It is time to remind yourself that you are well able to face whatever comes. As I write this, it has been only a few days since renowned basketball star Kobe Bryant and his daughter Gianni died in a helicopter crash along with seven other people. I'd only seen him play in a couple of live games, but my heart broke for his wife, Vanessa, and the resilience she will need in order to resume a "normal" life after such a huge loss.

(2) Trouble is required. It is the tool that produces spiritual, emotional, and psychological strength. You can liken trouble to what it takes to build physical muscles; that is, consistently resisting pressure. When we resist the temptation to feel that our trials are unfair and resist the pressure to respond in a negative way, we develop the "mental muscle" needed to overcome whatever obstacles arise. Handling problems is inherent in leadership—double that if you are a woman who must not only deal with the problems but also the expectations of how you should handle them.

(3) Trouble is seasonal. It will eventually pass. Do not adopt the mindset that you will always be stuck in your current negative circumstances. Never view a problem as insurmountable or impossible. Eliminate negative self-talk such as "I can't do this" or "This is too hard for me." Such declarations only reinforce erroneous beliefs. Instead, use empowering language

that inspires you to get back up. "This situation is working for my good." "There is a lesson in this!" You will be better served by analyzing the situation, asking for divine assistance, and anticipating a positive outcome.

- *Believe in the God who resides within you.* Often in the face of adversity, our self-esteem takes a hit. Don't allow any circumstances to make you feel less worthy. Your challenges do not define you. Adversity is just an experience; it is not your identity. Whatever happens, you are strong enough to regain control over your life. You simply need to remember that with God you can do all things.

- *Rely on your support network.* Everyone can get down occasionally. During these times, you can rely on your support network to cheer you on and encourage you to get back up again. Don't be afraid to ask for help. Rely on colleagues, friends, or loved ones to help get you through hard times. Challenges are easier to handle when we have someone to talk to. The people in our support group can remind us of who we are when adversity tempts us to forget. Nurture your support group and do not forget that support goes both ways. Be there for others during their trying times.

- *Don't be overly critical of yourself.* Beware of allowing your mistakes or any setback to define who you are. You are not a failure if you lose your job or get passed over for a high-profile role. You still have worth and value, and you just need to get back up and prove it. Every defeat gives you the chance to learn from your mistakes, if any, and be wiser in the future.

- *Don't be afraid to accept responsibility.* Sometimes adversity seems to come inexplicably out of the blue; other times, it comes as a result of our own actions. If you find that you have made unwise decisions, don't let this incapacitate you. Accept responsibility for your part in creating the problem and learn from your mistakes. Prepare a game plan to take those necessary next steps.

- *Don't neglect self-care.* Ironically, the key to resilience is first learning how to stop rather than forge ahead. In a 2014 paper, researchers Zijlstra, Cropley, and Rydstedt said that we need both internal and external recovery periods in order to build resilience.[3] Internal recovery periods are short breaks where we temporarily shift our attention from the work at hand. External recovery periods are longer breaks where we are completely removed from our work or tasks, such as after work, during weekends, and on holiday breaks.[4] It is essential to take care of your physical, mental, and spiritual health. Eating right, getting enough sleep, and exercising are critical. Most importantly, the time spent in the empowering presence of God and his Word will reap big dividends.

All problems are magnified when we are tired or stressed. It is critical that we take some downtime to replenish our reserves. Overworking significantly impacts the ability to be resilient, and we must allow ourselves a recovery period. Failure to do so results in increased incidences of health and safety problems. In her book *The Sleep Revolution*, Arianna Huffington says, "We sacrifice sleep in the name of productivity, but ironically, our loss of sleep, despite the extra hours we put in at work, adds up to more than eleven days of lost productivity per year per worker."[5] Overworking causes our bodies to be out of alignment, and thus we must expend more of our physical and mental resources to restore balance

We often underestimate our ability to recover from challenging situations, but most people are far more resilient than they give themselves credit for. Many of us have already made significant accomplishments that required resilience. Often, it's just a matter of looking back and evaluating past successes. Success in one area breeds confidence in other areas. It is often fear that holds us back from being either resilient or persistent; however, most situations aren't as bad as we think they are. They are certainly not too hard for our omnipotent God.

You are much more resilient than you give yourself credit for. You can leverage the confidence of past successes to pull you up and give you new energy to tackle life head-on. The popular saying "no pain, no gain" is often very true. Remember that most difficulties are temporary and provide the opportunity to learn and grow. William Arthur Ward once said, "Adversity causes some men to break; others, to break records."[6] The choice is up to you.

> **"Adversity causes some men to break; others, to break records."**

I must offer a word of caution regarding always forging ahead. It is important not to take persistence to the extreme. It may seem admirable to keep going when the odds are stacked against us, and being women who lead, we don't want to be labeled quitters. However, there are times when wisdom dictates that we let go of our dogged pursuit of a goal that is not part of God's plan. Even our tendency to be extremely merciful and enabling can be detrimental to someone's development and our own sanity. Be strong and seek God's will on when to throw in the towel on a futile effort.

8

FLEXIBLE:
Rolling with Changes and Challenges

*Blessed are the flexible, for they shall
not be bent out of shape.*
—Michael McGriffy, MD

Rigidity is a killer character trait—especially for a leader. Leadership styles can determine whether your team works together in harmony or whether the environment is filled with tension—whether there is resentment or camaraderie. When a leader's style clashes with those they lead, the result can be deflated morale and unproductivity. In any environment, being flexible is important.

Flexibility means being willing to adapt to changing circumstances and expectations. A flexible leader will work with her team to accommodate various personal needs while ensuring that responsibilities are not neglected. Flexibility also extends to giving leeway in the way a team works. An inflexible leader may be dogmatic not only in the work to be done but in how to accomplish it. A flexible leader is open to her team finding their own way to accomplish tasks, as long as the end result is achieved. She provides feedback and guidance when necessary but allows freedom in how to accomplish the job.

The ability to work from home continues to be more and more important to team members, and flexible leaders embrace this cultural shift when it is feasible to do so. Even if it isn't possible to allow people to work from home year-round, you may be able to offer this option a couple of days a week. Another cultural change that has become a norm is implementing a flexible work schedule, which involves letting a team set their own start and end times—within reason.

Female Leaders Uniquely More Flexible

Female leaders are often more flexible than their male counterparts. Gallup reports that women outperform men in developing an engaged team—that is, people who are enthusiastic about and committed to their leader and their work. The study found that those who report to female leaders are more likely to agree with the following statements:

- *There is someone at work who encourages my development.* Female leaders are likely to take more interest in developing their team to help them reach their full potential.

- *In the last six months, someone has talked to me about my progress.* Women may be more likely to provide regular feedback on the progress of team members than men.

- *In the last seven days, I have received recognition or praise for doing good work.* Giving positive feedback that makes the team feel valued is often easier for women than for men.[1]

Many women in the marketplace have demonstrated flexibility and impacted their organization's bottom line. Take Susan Wojcicki, for example. She established herself as a tech visionary at Google. She was the senior vice-president of advertising and commerce and was responsible for the launching of Google Analytics. When she learned that YouTube was competing against Google's video service, she proposed an acquisition and orchestrated the $1.65 billion purchase in 2006. Susan became YouTube's CEO in 2014. The site's value increased exponentially under her leadership. She credits her success to her flexibility and willingness to adapt to new situations.[2] "Things are always changing. Part of being successful here is being comfortable with not knowing what's going to happen," she told *The New York Times*.[3]

Negative Aspects of Being Too Flexible

Being flexible without having a plan or seeing the big picture can backfire and result in team members who do what they want with no accountability. While flexibility in a leader is important, here are some things to beware of with this approach:

- *Focusing on an immediate need rather than a long-term need.* Sometimes a team member's immediate need is not beneficial for the company's overall long-term objectives. Trying to accommodate everyone's specific needs can backfire and cause leaders to fall into the trap of trying to take care of their team instead of effectively running the company and meeting key deadlines.

- *Not being specific.* Being flexible doesn't mean being non-specific in your requests. If you want something done, it's best to give specific guidance and say exactly what you mean. You can then offer flexibility in how to accomplish the given task. Being specific reduces the chances of receiving work that isn't what you envisioned. Your team can't read your mind, so it's best to provide as much detail as possible about your expectations.

- *Letting people off the hook for bad behavior.* Sometimes women, in particular, allow bad behavior or poor performance in the name of being flexible. While it is true that everyone has weaknesses, you must hold people accountable for their work and for their development.

- *Failing to adjust leadership style when appropriate.* Some women use the same leadership style regardless of the person or the situation. Flexible leaders have the unique challenge of determining whether that leadership style is hampering a particular team member rather than enhancing them. Flexibility is a benefit that can and should be taken away if someone is taking advantage of it. Offer flexibility only when basic expectations are being met.

- *Failing to evaluate yourself.* Are you being flexible or are you being a pushover? Often the two can look similar; therefore, it is necessary to evaluate the motives behind your behavior. For example, are you making certain decisions because you want people to like and accept you? Do you have trouble being direct? In both cases, you are hiding behind the guise of flexibility and need to address the underlying issues.[4]

Steps to Becoming a More Flexible Leader

The most effective leader is one who can modify their management style to accommodate people with a variety of strengths, backgrounds, personalities, and work styles. While women normally possess this attribute, there is always room for improvement. The following are some steps you can implement to become more flexible in your leadership style:

- *Evaluate your team:* You need to understand the way your team members work, which means asking the right questions, such as "How can I best help you succeed?," "How much feedback do you require in order to know whether you are on the right track?," and "Do you prefer to make decisions autonomously or would you rather obtain my guidance and approval before moving forward?"[5]

- *Develop a plan:* Your plan should include how often you will meet with each team member, how much direction you will provide when assigning projects, and how you will hold them accountable. It's important to set firm guidelines while being flexible enough to make changes as needed.

- *Reassess periodically:* Evaluate your plan and determine whether it is working as you envisioned. Are you seeing an improvement in the work habits of your team, or are they unproductive? Also, check in with your team for their input on how things are going from their point of view.[6]

- *Assess your flexibility:* You can assess how flexible you are by asking the following questions:

  - Have I considered alternate approaches to solving a problem?

  - Am I open to trying new suggestions or strategies from others?

  - Can I recognize when changes to my behavior are needed?

- *Don't automatically dismiss advice:* You may think you know best how to handle a problem or get a job done. After all, you're the leader for a reason. However, it is important to be the kind of leader who listens to and evaluates all advice and feedback. No one is perfect, and others may have a different perspective that you hadn't thought of.

- *Expect the unexpected:* Good leaders know that not everything goes the way they plan. You must be willing and able to keep a clear head when conflicts and problems arise so you can deal with them in the most appropriate way.

Being a great leader requires the ability to manage your team based on their unique strengths, levels of experience, and individual styles and preferences. When you can be flexible and adapt to changing circumstances, you enable your team to be motivated and effective. Notwithstanding, you must be careful not to take flexibility too far. Being too flexible can result in problems within your team if there is no accountability. Implement continuous feedback and enforce consequences for missed deadlines and other poor work habits. As a leader, you will want the workplace culture to be a positive one, but remember that your team must also earn your flexibility and understanding.

When you can be flexible and adapt to changing circumstances, you enable your team to be motivated and effective.

VULNERABLE:
Getting Real About Your Weaknesses

To share your weakness is to make yourself vulnerable;
to make yourself vulnerable is to show your strength.

—Criss Jami, American poet

"Genny," an ambitious African American woman in her mid-forties, is a ranking officer on the fast track in the police department of a large city. She regularly volunteers to work an insane number of overtime hours—even on weekends, which her outdoors-loving husband "Edward" considers sacred family time. All her life, Genny has been told that as a minority, she must work twice as hard to gain half the recognition or reward. Edward resents her obsession with work and has rebelled by becoming emotionally unavailable. He confided to a close friend that he secretly desires to be her "knight in shining armor"; however, he lamented that she is so self-sufficient that she never gives him the opportunity to rescue her from any adversity. One night, her car broke down a few miles from their home. When she called to inform him of her plight, without forethought, he replied, "Call AAA" (the Automobile Association of America, which renders roadside emergency service). Not having a clue that her call was an indirect request to be rescued, or at least to be emotionally supported, he was totally baffled when she burst into tears. Genny was not a crier; she was as tough as nails and could resolve any problem that came her way. Edward had never witnessed her being so vulnerable during the entire 10 years of their marriage. Further, not being emotionally savvy, he didn't rationalize that she had deemed his response cold and uncaring. *Surely*, he had thought, *she knows that AAA is better equipped to handle the stalled car.* The last I heard, Edward and Genny were heading to divorce court. I wonder what the outcome of their marriage would have been had she shown more vulnerability and had he been more sensitive to her needs.

Although vulnerability is a stereotypical label applied to women, it is a trait that we would be wise to embrace as an asset in our personal and professional lives—especially when it comes to leadership.

Why Vulnerability Works

You saw in Genny's case how adopting a "Wonder Woman" persona can be alienating in personal relationships. However, it can be especially counterproductive in your role as a leader. It sets you up in a superior position, putting a wall between you and the fallible people you lead—making you unrelatable, untouchable, and excludable from key "grapevine" or inside information that could prove vital to your effectiveness. Unfortunately, the fear of appearing weak will hold many women captive. Yet we as women are socially permitted to show vulnerability, since we do not normally have super egos to protect or a macho image to maintain. Nevertheless, women on the fast track are still frequently admonished to avoid displaying vulnerability in our professional environments and to reserve such disclosures for discussion with family or close friends. We are cautioned that to do otherwise is the kiss of death to developing an image as a strong woman. Don't buy into the myth; vulnerability is not the kiss of death. In fact, Brené Brown, famed researcher and bestselling author of *Daring Greatly,* asserts that vulnerability is the best measure of courage. She defines it as "the willingness to show up and be seen by others in the face of uncertain outcomes" and declares that "there's not a single act of courage that doesn't involve vulnerability."[1]

Consider the following benefits of being vulnerable:

- *Vulnerability relieves us of the stress of wearing our perfection or achievement mask.* In this fast-moving information age, there is way too much to know and to stay abreast of. The only way to survive is to rely on the combined knowledge of your followers, staff, or others. That's as true at work as it is in our personal lives. "Vulnerability is the birthplace of innovation, creativity, and change," Brené says. "If you've created a work culture where vulnerability isn't okay, you've also created a culture where innovation and creativity aren't okay."[2] When you lead like a woman, you don't fear shining the light on your weaknesses or shortcomings. In so doing, you free others of the stress of pretending to know it all.

- *Vulnerability helps us own our weaknesses and challenges.* Once we acknowledge and accept them, we can stop denying or trying to justify them. If our weaknesses impact people around us in a negative way, we can develop strategies and solicit accountability partners to help us eliminate them. For example, having a high energy, Type-A personality, I find it hard to sit in long meetings without nodding off—which can be quite embarrassing. So when possible, I try to sit next to someone I know and ask them to kindly give me a nudge if they see me dozing. This works great—unless they have the same problem!

- *Vulnerability permits us to receive and extend compassion.* Since showing our vulnerability humanizes us, we become more likely to look beyond the faults or shortcomings of others and consider their circumstances. And since we reap what we sow, others are more likely to reciprocate the response. If we have never given anyone an inkling of our personal circumstances, people will simply judge our professional behavior based on their own assumptions. Before my elderly mother passed away, she suffered from dementia. On a few occasions, I had to bring her to wait in my office at the company where I worked until one of my siblings could pick her up. My staff was quick to respond with games, Play-Doh, and other time-filling distractions until relief arrived. When they had family or other personal issues that needed their time and attention, I gladly approved their time off and offered to help in any way possible. Our mutual vulnerabilities created a strong, tightly knit group in our department.

Vulnerability permits us to receive
and extend compassion.

- *Modeling vulnerability shows others how to be vulnerable.* When we have the courage to reveal who we really are and the weaknesses that we battle, we not only gain credibility but also create a safe space where others are free to follow our example. Opportunities to be vulnerable present themselves every day and include such things as saying, "I'm sorry, I made a mistake"; "I don't know"; "I need your input on this problem"; and "I'm very fortunate to have you on my team."

Managing Vulnerability

Despite the benefits of being vulnerable, as with all our inherent feminine leadership traits, this too must be managed so that this asset doesn't become a liability. Since one of the laws of human nature is that people connect more quickly with our weaknesses and vulnerabilities than our strengths and competencies, we may be tempted to try to fast-track the process by becoming too vulnerable. Don't do it. Too much vulnerability too soon can backfire on you.

Many years ago, when I took a job with a community nonprofit, I sought a connection with the only other female on the management team. We professed a similar faith in God, so I assumed we could have an iron-sharpens-iron relationship. One day I said to her, "Let's be mutually accountable to each other. If you observe any behavior on my part that you think may be a blind spot or detriment to the organization or to my effectiveness here, I give you permission to let me know." We agreed to be mutually accountable. Over several months, we shared areas of our lives where we were personally and professionally challenged. Soon, I began to hear rumors that she had spoken negatively about me to some of our coworkers. Even the CEO revealed that she had made negative remarks about me to him—and about him to others. I was infuriated by her betrayal. Rather than confront her—which would have been my normal modus operandi—I decided to let it go as a lesson learned. From that point on, I kept the relationship on a surface level. Since that and other similar experiences, I've learned several lessons about managing vulnerability:

- *Don't share too soon.* Take time to observe the character and conversation of the people you plan to share with. Consider the nature and depth of your relationship before you introduce personal information.

- *Consider the potential impact of what you plan to reveal.* Ask yourself, "If someone were to share with me the weakness I'm about to share, how would it affect my perception of them?" This is not to say you should pretend to be perfect. It's simply using wisdom in what you communicate. When I took a job as the CFO of a megachurch, I was not proficient in the mechanics of operating their accounting system. When the key accounting supervisor found a better career opportunity, I hired a female consultant to take over the role temporarily. Moved by envy, she took great delight in telling one of my staff members that I didn't "have a clue" about the system. I refused to allow her critical remark to faze me. My job was not to record transactions but to oversee and manage the people, the process, and the profit-and-loss statements the system produced. I had already informed my staff that I did not know the inner workings of the system. I was confident that I could excel in the more complicated aspects of the job—including successfully negotiating the landmark financing to construct the multimillion-dollar cathedral.

- *Don't share too much info.* You may desire to be viewed as a transparent leader, but guard against extreme or embarrassing personal revelations. I attended a female awards luncheon once where one of the awardees recounted the obstacles she had faced to excel in her job. She gave a blow-by-blow account of having her first child: "My water broke en route to work" (TMI [too much information]—especially for a mixed audience!). The men in the room looked uncomfortable. Further, that piece of information was not relevant, inspiring, or empathy-generating to the audience. Don't fall into the trap of simply talking too much.

  Here are a few examples of what's off-limits for sharing in your role as a leader or influencer: your husband's career failures or financial shortcomings, how grateful you are that you found favor with the boss in light of your limited experience, or the details of a personal surgery. Of course, I often tell the story of my 14 months of excruciating pain that ultimately resulted in my having brain surgery, which threatened to topple my speaking career before it could get off the ground. My goal is to inspire people to press through and defy the odds—and most of all to have faith for a miracle.

- *Don't use vulnerability to manipulate.* Sometimes we may be tempted to share weaknesses in order to level the playing field so that we are not perceived as "privileged" or "preferred" over others—particularly other women. This is especially true when you have a reputation for being extremely competent or enjoy a personal connection with a powerful person in the organization (such as being the CEO's daughter, a pastor's relative, a graduate of a prestigious university, the most credentialed person on staff, etc.). Such a position can automatically set you up for rejection due to envy—no matter how humble you are.

  You may be tempted to share the details of your childhood troubles or other personal woes to evoke sympathy hoping it could lead to favor in some way. Or consider the woman who feigns helplessness or ignorance so that the men around her can have the satisfaction of having their egos massaged by rescuing her. In so doing, she unwittingly teaches them to view her as not being an equal or having the potential to be. Of course, this is not a call to reject a man's offer to lift heavy packages nor to rebuff him for other practical overtures. Many men have been taught to be gentlemen, and it is part of their core behavior. A wise woman will appreciate that and graciously accept assistance.

  My admonition here is simply to be honest about your "why" for being vulnerable. Know that most people can smell inauthenticity a mile away. Therefore, do not even think about faking it.

There is no need to fear being vulnerable. Rather than expecting your superiors, colleagues, or subordinates to take advantage of you, know that you are wisely positioning yourself to gain increased connection, loyalty, and respect. You have demonstrated that you are a leader with the courage to be authentic—as well as freeing those you lead to be so. In the final analysis, divine strength is made perfect and manifested in our weaknesses. The apostle Paul sought God's healing from an infirmity only to have God respond with a "no" on three different occasions. "Each time he said, 'My grace is all you need. My power works best in weakness.' So now I am glad to boast about my weaknesses, so that the power of Christ can work through me. That's why I take pleasure in my weaknesses.... For when I am weak, then I am strong" (2 Corinthians 12:9-10).

Yes, this is the paradox of being vulnerable: It makes you strong.

SERVANT-HEARTED:
Unveiling the Secret to Greatness

*Those who are the greatest among you should take the
lowest rank, and the leader should be like a servant.*

Luke 22:26

Leadership begins with service, and no one is more service-oriented than a woman. Robert K. Greenleaf coined the term *servant leadership*, saying that it "begins with the natural feeling that one wants to serve, to serve *first*. Then conscious choice brings one to aspire to lead."[1] And although Greenleaf coined the term, Jesus coined the concept and explained it to his glory-seeking disciples. "Then they began to argue among themselves about who would be the greatest among them. Jesus told them, 'In this world the kings and great men lord it over their people, yet they are called "friends of the people." But among you it will be different. Those who are the greatest among you should take the lowest rank, and the leader should be like a servant.'"[2] Jesus did not measure greatness by the number of people who served him but by the number of people he served.

The effectiveness of a servant leader is not measured by rank or position, rather it's measured by the legacy the leader leaves behind. All leaders should ask themselves, "Does my leadership cause personal and professional growth in others?"

Servant leaders submit themselves to others voluntarily and not under compulsion. Jesus washed the disciples' feet, cast out demons, and chastised the Pharisees when he deemed necessary. He was a strong leader. Servant leaders give selflessly without expecting anything in return. Doesn't this sound like the natural tendency of most females? Since the servant leadership style exhibits the same behavior required to be a good mother, wife, caregiver, or other nurturing functions, women easily excel in this style.

Servant leaders seek to know the following of those they lead: *What are your aspirations? What are your key motivations? How can I help you get from here to there?* Because servant leadership embraces self-giving without self-glory, it is an ideal leadership style. Let's look at a few of the benefits and cautions of this style.

––––––––––––––––

Because servant leadership embraces self-giving without self-glory, it is an ideal leadership style.

––––––––––––––––

Benefits of Servant Leadership

It's Not About Just One Person: Many leaders focus on their best interests rather than on the needs of the many. However, servant leaders make decisions that are in the best interest of the organization as a whole rather than just one or two people.

It Improves the Work Culture: Many of us have worked for different companies during our careers, and we can attest that some work cultures are more pleasing than others. When the person at the top is a servant leader, it affects the atmosphere and the people who work there in a positive manner.

It Promotes Customer Retention: Customers often do not know what's going on behind the scenes in an organization, but they can feel the effects of poor leadership. When employees are unhappy, they pass that on to the customers they serve. In the same way, when employees are happy and love what they do, customers naturally want to do business with them.

It Promotes Innovation: Nothing is more disheartening than to feel that your ideas don't count. For this reason, servant leaders keep an open mind when their subordinates suggest new ways of doing things. They don't agree just for the sake of agreeing, but they genuinely consider and embrace those things that would enhance the organization as a whole.

It Keeps the Ego in Check: In a traditional leadership role, the person in charge makes all the decisions, communicates what needs to be done, and then takes credit for the completed project. On the other hand, servant leaders give credit where credit is due to help others reach higher standards of performance.

Cautions of Servant Leadership

Servant leadership has its downside, which can include the following.

Lack of Motivation: Servant leaders may hamper those they lead by solving every problem and always coming to the rescue. This is especially true for female leaders, who are nurturing by nature. When issues arise, it might be easier for some people to just let the servant leader handle it rather than taking the initiative to handle issues on their own.

Lack of Respect: Some people believe leaders should be tough. If you are a servant leader, some people may take that as a sign of weakness and think they can take advantage of your good nature. They see your leadership style as lacking in authority. Servant leaders must learn to exert authority while still serving their people well.

More Time-Consuming: Servant leaders must consider others rather than just making decisions and forcing people to live with them. Therefore, it can take longer to make decisions and get things done. Servant leaders must walk the fine line of caring for those they lead while making the best decision for the organization they serve.

Many of the world's leading corporations and brands have demonstrated that they understand the power of putting people ahead of profits. While they do care about their companies' bottom line, they care more about those who work and serve with them.

Cheryl Bachelder, author of the book *Dare to Serve: How to Drive Superior Results by Serving Others*, is the CEO of Popeyes Louisiana Kitchen. In 2007, Popeyes was in bad shape. Customer retention had been steadily declining, the stock price had dropped from $34 to $13, and sales had plummeted. However, Cheryl managed to reinvent the company from the inside out. Just seven years later, in 2014, sales increased by 25 percent, the stock price soared to more than $40, and profits had increased by 40 percent. As a result, franchisees once again began investing in the company, building new restaurants, and remodeling existing ones.[3]

Cheryl explained, "We needed to serve the people who have invested the most in Popeyes."[4] She decided to create a new work culture "where people were treated with respect and dignity, yet challenged to perform at the highest level." She listened to those who owned the restaurants and responded to their needs while letting go of self-serving leaders. Customers became more loyal to the company because their experience was more rewarding and satisfying. In 2015, Cheryl was given the Norman Award, which recognizes leaders who have made a significant impact on their peers.[5]

The Test of a Servant Leader

How are you doing as a servant leader? Perhaps you see yourself in that role, but how do others see you? Are you serving well and leading well? What will people say about you after they leave your leadership? Here are some questions to ask when considering your effectiveness as a servant leader:

- If people had the choice to have you lead them again, would they choose you?

- Are you using people to accomplish your own goals rather than working together to accomplish the goals of the organization?

- Are your followers learning and growing under your leadership? Are you helping them reach their full potential?

- Do your subordinates feel valued? Do you recognize them and appreciate them?

- Do you serve your people or merely try to impress your superiors?

- Are you pouring into people such that any one of them could replace you if you left?

- Do you give credit where credit is due and thank people for a job well done?

The essence of Jesus's leadership is demonstrated in those he left behind. After he washed his disciples' feet, he said to them, "Now that I, your Lord and Teacher, have washed your feet, you also should wash one another's feet. I have set you an example that you should do as I have done for you" (John 13:14-15 NIV). So how did his disciples perform after he left? Did they successfully use everything he had taught them? The answer is a resounding yes. Without their efforts, Christianity would have died with Jesus Christ instead of spreading to the four corners of the earth.

Many leaders would rather rule than serve. Authority often brings with it power and prestige, while being a servant is often seen as being weak and powerless. However, this is far from the truth. Servant leadership is not passive, nor is it a way for people to hide when they don't have the courage or ability to lead. It doesn't mean keeping everyone happy and doing everything they want. On the contrary, servant leadership requires two components: the first is that one be a *servant* but the other is that one be a *leader*. Servant leaders are not soft people who can't get anything done. They are responsible to lead as well as any other type of leader.

Dr. Shirley Mullen, president of Houghton College is a servant leader. During our interview, she shared her personal experience of assuming her role.

Me: What was the biggest hurdle you had to overcome in assuming your position?

Dr. Mullen: My biggest hurdle was learning to lead while knowing that a major part of my organization did not want me in the leadership position. I had always been used to being affirmed at every turn. Learning to lead while knowing that others do not support you—or affirm what you are doing—was a major mental hurdle. I overcame it by realizing that I had been called to this role, both by God and the board of trustees—and by learning that I did not need to have everyone's approval to move forward. Only go forward if you love the work and feel called. Do not need or fall in love with the position. Always hold your position lightly so that you are free to make the decisions that you truly believe are the best ones for the institution. Do not let yourself get to the point where you are hedging on presenting your best judgments because you are trying to protect your position.

J. Oswald Sanders said, "True greatness, true leadership, is found in giving yourself in service to others, not in coaxing or inducing others to serve you."[6] And John R.W. Stott declared, "Leaders have power, but power is safe only in the hands of those who humble themselves to serve."[7] Philippians 2:3-5 sums up the proper attitude of a servant leader when it says that we should do nothing out of selfish ambition or vain conceit. Instead, we must be humble and consider others better than ourselves. We must look not only to our own interests but also the interests of others.

Whenever you feel like elevating yourself, remember the example of Jesus. Philippians 2:6-7 (NIV) says that he was "in very nature God," yet he did not use this to his advantage. Instead, he took on human nature and the nature of a servant. His mission was not to be served but to serve and to give his life as a ransom for many (Mark 10:45).

11

PRINCIPLED:
Being a Values-Driven Leader

*I wouldn't ask anyone to do anything
I wouldn't do myself.*

—Indra Nooyi, CEO of PepsiCo

Queen Jezebel, the wife of Ahab, king of Israel, was a leader devoid of godly principles. She orchestrated the death of a landowner after he refused to sell Ahab a parcel of land. She killed the prophets of God. She was the exception to the research that shows "men tend to have more lenient ethical standards than women."[1] In the end, God punished her for all her evil deeds and the dogs devoured her after one of her disloyal servants threw her from a window (read her story in 1 Kings 16–2 Kings 9). What a legacy! How do you wish to be remembered? Have you committed yourself and your organization to high moral principles that inform your actions?

Many companies display signs in their hallways and common areas that proclaim their core values. Values are qualities or traits that represent one's priorities and convictions. They keep the leader and the corporation accountable. I know of a very popular organization whose core values include the importance of the family and work-life balance. Therefore, it is their policy to allow employee overtime only when absolutely necessary. Their personnel policies are also family friendly.

When women are part of the executive team or when they serve on company boards, there will usually be a higher level of sensitivity to embracing such core values. Organizations that are effective, customer-centric, and employee-oriented develop a clear, concise, and shared meaning about their values, beliefs, priorities, and direction. They want every employee to understand the values, strive to emulate the values, contribute to the values, and model the values. Once defined, the values should impact every aspect of an organization.

Your personal value system is important in the corporate culture because employees tend to bring their values to the organization. As employees mingle with others, each with their own values, they eventually integrate their values and end up forming an organizational culture. The culture that is formed will either benefit the organization or make it harder to achieve its objectives. In cases where the culture formed is counterproductive, ingenious ways must be devised to redefine the organizational culture in order to create a beneficial culture.

Key Values to Embrace

An organization's core values run the gamut from collaboration, diversity, innovation, teamwork, and accountability to flexibility, service, environmentalism, loyalty, frugality, and more. Here are a few key values every organization would benefit from embracing:

Excellence

Excellence is intentional. Anyone who excels at anything in life does so because they made a deliberate effort. Excellence is one of the most important values and yet one of the most deficient in modern corporate culture. Many allow the interesting things around them to distract them from what's important. They do not focus on the task at hand. Consequently, the quality of output is usually wanting. The apostle Paul exhorted us to work "heartily" as unto the Lord and not as unto man.[2] It is a good habit upon completing any endeavor to pause and ask yourself if God would be happy with the output. The goal is to strive for excellence. Caution: Excellence is by no means the same as perfection. No one is perfect, and perfectionism can be detrimental to productivity. Having the spirit of excellence means being willing to do ordinary things extraordinarily well. Perfectionism will drain you but excellence will rejuvenate you. We will delve deeper into the perils of perfectionism in chapter 14.

Integrity

A person of integrity is one who sticks to her principles no matter what, one whose moral compass isn't broken. She realizes that doing the right thing might cost her, but she does not allow a negative consequence to keep her from doing it. The lack of integrity is displayed every day in corporate culture. For instance, it is not uncommon for a supervisor to take all the credit for a successful project even though he knew he had nothing to do with it. A boss that has integrity will share the spotlight with their junior staff who made it possible. A boss that walks in integrity refuses to engage in power plays with their colleagues. Another good illustration of integrity is a woman that refuses to give in to the sexual demands of a boss even though he is promising a promotion in return. A woman of integrity will realize that any promotion that doesn't come through her genuine hard work and merit isn't worth it.

Communication

Most companies claim to value open communication, but if their individual employees don't value it, the overall organizational culture will lack it. Even though an organization can survive without open communication, it wouldn't be possible for the organization to really thrive without it. The foundation of open communication is trust. It is quite difficult to communicate openly with someone you do not trust. For instance, when customers are not sure how a company will use their private data, they will be very reluctant to share it, even if it is for their own good. When employees engage and communicate openly, it means they are free and care for their work. But for this to happen, a company must demonstrate that they also value and care for their employees. Employees who feel valued by their organization feel more motivated to show up for work and give their best. Otherwise, they will only give their bare minimum.

Optimism

Optimism, like any other value, is something that we learn based on our environment. This is important because even if you were raised to be a "glass-half-empty" kind of a person, you can still learn to adopt a "glass-half-full" mind-set. Optimism in business and career goes a long way. People who have a positive outlook on life are happier and more fulfilled and eventually live longer. Optimistic people do not need a reason to be happy—they can turn any situation into something good. Optimists will find an oasis in every desert of calamity. You too can be optimistic—just start by listing the things you are thankful for or, as the hymnist put it, "Count your many blessings; name them one by one." Try writing them down. As you focus on the positives, the negatives just may begin looking more insignificant.

Your Values, Your Choice

Your value system is a culmination of everything that has happened to you in your lifetime. It will most likely be developed by your family, parents, religious affiliation, education, reading, friends, and peers. If you are to be effective in anything, you must start by realizing that your values were influenced by many environmental factors. This is important because it helps to isolate and prioritize the most important values. Once you define your values, they will inform your leadership priorities.

Walking in integrity can be a challenge, and according to research, women are more likely to do so than men. Professor Laura Kray of UC Berkley noticed from her MBA students that the men took a more lenient approach to ethics than the women, who were more principled.[3] In the corporate world, women have to deal with all manner of compromising situations as they forge their way in the corporate jungle. There are a number of possible explanations, but generally, women are often looked at as sexual objects by their male counterparts. The victims of harassment rarely speak out due to fear or embarrassment. Their silence allows the vice to flourish unchecked. Sex is often used as a tool of career advancement and even though women are more principled, some end up giving in for fear of losing promotion opportunities or, worse still, their jobs.

As a woman, please be reminded that any suggestion by anyone for sexual favors in exchange for promotion is not only immoral and inappropriate but also illegal. You are well within your right to seek legal recourse should your boss engage in any inappropriate behavior toward you.

Yes, you may have colleagues at the office that give in to the demands of powerful, influential men. They may even appear to benefit from such arrangements. But you don't have to compromise your values. Hold on to your integrity and refuse to bow to the pressure.

Managing the Trait: Principled Versus Rigid

A story is told of a reed and an oak and how the two responded to a strong wind. The oak remained sturdy and unmoved, while the reed bent and swayed in the wind. Eventually, the oak was blown over by the wind, while the reed remained firmly in position. The oak wondered why the reed didn't fall as it had even though it had a weaker stem. The reed explained, "You can't stop the wind from blowing. And when the wind starts to blow, those who are stubborn cannot withstand the assault. But those who are adaptable and humble will withstand the wind."

This story reveals an important truth about being principled—it doesn't necessarily mean that you must be rigid. You can adapt to situations without compromising your values. One simple way of doing this is ensuring you live by principles rather than rules. Rules are rigid, and they are based on absolutes, authority, and hierarchy. Principles, however, are founded on mindful living and flexibility. Instead of being absolute, they call for contemplation, which makes it easier to apply. We follow rules because we are afraid of the consequences of breaking the rules, but the same cannot be said of principles. Principles are based on values and can, therefore, affect every decision we make, consciously or subconsciously.

>You can adapt to situations without
>compromising your values.

You can never go wrong holding fast to your personal code of conduct, but don't go overboard and judge or condemn those who do not embrace your beliefs. When you are adamant about standing on convictions, be honest about your motivation. Do you really hold certain convictions, or are you following traditions or trying to solidify your judgmental position atop a pedestal. Now, if your organization holds that high morals are part of the driving values, fine. But in a secular workplace, your most effective individual approach will be to model a good example. Don't laugh at the off-color jokes, and for goodness' sake, don't tell one just to fit in. Having strong convictions is healthy as long as you're convicted by the truth and not your pride, ego, or tradition.

RESOURCEFUL:
Finding a Way to Succeed

*I like to say it's an attitude of not just thinking
outside the box, but not even seeing the box.*

—Safra A. Catz, CEO of Oracle Corporation

She is nameless among the women profiled in the Old Testament, but with one targeted drop of a piece of an upper millstone from the top of a strong tower, the woman of Thebez saved the lives of all the inhabitants of her city. Their adversary, the heartless, power-hungry King Abimelech was about to set fire to the door of the tower—just as he had recently done in the city of Shechem, where he had burned 1,000 men and women alive as they sought refuge in a temple. This woman had no delegated authority. She was not the head of Homeland Security or even his administrative assistant. She had no time to seek permission or approval from higher-ups for her proposed actions. The town was in a life-or-death crisis. She used her resourcefulness and threw down the millstone piece that crushed Abimelech's skull—and his pride. The absurdity of it all is that the king's chief concern was what people would say when they learned the manner of his death. "Then he called quickly to the young man, his armor-bearer, and said to him, 'Draw your sword and kill me, lest men say of me, "A woman killed him."' So his young man thrust him through, and he died."[1]

Where There Is a Woman, There Is a Way

Resourcefulness is one of the many inherent leadership traits in which women excel. It is the ability to find creative ways to solve problems. When faced with challenges, resourceful women look outside the box for solutions. They confront adverse circumstances with ingenuity and passion. Women often see what others do not and know how to connect the dots to embrace new opportunities. "Many women leaders find excitement and motivation by being extremely creative and resourceful when completing tasks and other duties and responsibilities."[2] Resourceful women exhibit the following qualities:

- They are flexible in how they approach a problem or situation.

- They are not constrained by how they were initially taught to seek solutions.

- They work hard and don't expect things to be handed to them.

- They don't mind asking for help, understanding that their network and contacts might know something they do not.

- They are unwilling to compromise what they believe in.

- They turn challenges into advantages.

- They remain calm in the face of pressure.

- They can execute complex business models and strategies.

- They are open-minded and don't mind overcoming obstacles. Women don't mind moving outside of their comfort zone and forsaking tradition if it will advance their progress.

Women don't mind moving outside of
their comfort zone and forsaking tradition
if it will advance their progress.

- They believe in the impossible. They don't give up even when things are hard. Failure and frustration simply fuel them to succeed. They know every failure brings them one step closer to success.

- They play more than one hand. If one option doesn't work, another may.

- They believe there is a solution to every problem.

- They are imaginative and creative.

- They are proactive; they don't wait for just the right person or just the right resource to present itself.

- They are hopeful and remain positive, even if it means they must change direction.

- They never stop educating themselves and are thus able to stay ahead of the game in their respective industries.

- They don't procrastinate but get things done when it's necessary.

Why Resourcefulness Matters

"Resourcefulness is a mindset, and is especially relevant when the goals you have set are difficult to achieve or you cannot envision a clear path to get to where you desire to go…An attitude of resourcefulness inspires out-of-the-box thinking, the generation of new ideas, and the ability to visualize all the possible ways to achieve what you desire."[3]

One benefit of resourcefulness that may be surprising is that it enhances self-development, self-improvement, and self-worth. It helps you reflect on your current skills and determine if there are any you need to strengthen or develop. All these involve the resolve and resilience of the human spirit. In the book *Coach Wooden's Pyramid of Success*, legendary basketball coach John Wooden says,

> Resourcefulness is using our wits, proper judgment and common sense to solve problems and meet challenges.

> It is using initiative in difficult situations and involves
> inventing, creating, imagining, synthesizing, evaluating,
> classifying, observing and analyzing solutions to over-
> come the trials that life throws at us. Resourcefulness is
> dreaming up ways to meet our goals.[4]

John Wooden had to be resourceful when he lived in a fraternity
house at Purdue University. He had trouble studying because there
was always so much noise, so he decided to start getting up at 3 a.m.
to accomplish the task in peace and quiet. When he needed money,
he had to put his resourcefulness to use again, selling food at football
games and selling basketball programs during the basketball season.
He says that most people would call this an entrepreneurial spirit, but
he just saw it as being resourceful.[5]

You may remember the old TV show *MacGyver*. In every episode,
the lead character, who had the unlikely name of Angus MacGyver,
used his ingenuity to get himself out of some pretty tough situations. He applied his technological and scientific knowledge to life-
or-death situations where he was always racing against the clock or
had limited resources. He routinely accomplished seemingly impossible feats such as disarming bombs with a paper clip, using duct tape
to get himself out of dangerous circumstances, and making repairs
with chewing gum. We can learn a lot about resourcefulness from
MacGyver's escapades.

Here are some questions you can ask yourself to ensure you are
making the most of every situation:

- Is there another way to get what I want? (If your current
  plan does not work, what is plan B?)

- Is my desired outcome really what's best? (You may be
  going down a wrong path and need to course correct.)

- Who else has the information I need? (You may not have
  all the answers, but there is always someone who does.
  Find that person.)

Resourceful Female Leaders

Resourcefulness is a mind-set, and to be successful, women must embody characteristics such as discipline, dedication, hard work, confidence, and willingness. Resourceful women are extraordinary thinkers. If they don't know the answer, they know how to get it. As Ernest Hemingway said, "Now is no time to think of what you do not have. Think of what you can do with what there is." History is filled with women who used their resourcefulness to get ahead.

Estée Lauder

Estée Lauder was a legend in the cosmetics industry who got her start selling her uncle's cosmetic creams and lotions to her friends. In 1946, she officially formed Estée Lauder Cosmetics Inc., achieving her first breakthrough when Saks Fifth Avenue ordered $800 worth of her products and sold out within two days. Lauder's company evolved into various cosmetic lines such as MAC, Aramis, and Clinique. "Lauder was as innovative with her marketing strategies as her cosmetic products, eventually making her the richest self-made woman in the world."[6] When her company went public in 1995, it was valued at approximately $2 billion.

Lauder demonstrated her resourcefulness particularly after the war when women indicated a desire to sample products before purchasing them. She rose to the demand and pioneered two marketing tactics that are popular today: the free sample and free gift with purchase. Lauder once said, "I never dreamed about success. I worked for it."[7]

Ida B. Wells-Barnett

Born into slavery during the Civil War, journalist and activist Ida B. Wells-Barnett battled sexism, racism, and violence in her lifetime. She used her journalism skills to shed light on the conditions of African Americans in the South. Ida attended Rust College but was expelled when she had a disagreement with the university president. After yellow fever took the lives of both her parents and her infant brother, she had to care for her brothers and sisters, taking a job as a teacher to do so.

Ida had fought for various causes over her lifetime. She sued a company for unfairly throwing her off a first-class train and she investigated several cases of the lynching of black men and published her findings in newspapers and pamphlets. As a result of one exposé, her press was burned down, and she was driven away from Memphis by unhappy citizens. Ida was one of the founders of the National Association of Colored Women's Club, which addressed women's suffrage and civil rights issues. While Ida is not given the recognition she deserves, she was also a founding member of the National Association for the Advancement of Colored People (NAACP).

The Proverbs 31 Woman

In the Bible, the Proverbs 31 woman is the epitome of resourcefulness. She is described as a woman of excellence in whom her family can place their full confidence. She is a hardworking woman who takes initiative and possesses great strength and courage. She is resourceful with whatever is placed in her hand, skilled in using wool and flax to make clothing for her household. She is a woman of influence, managing her household, servants, money, and land well. The Proverbs 31 woman is both a shrewd seller and a shrewd buyer, and she plans to avoid unforeseen calamities. Most importantly, she fears the Lord, and the text says such a woman is more valuable than rubies.[8]

Those who don't have the trait of resourcefulness accept defeat because they believe obstacles cannot be overcome. They are unable to imagine and unable to create. Resourceful women find a way to achieve their goals. They are skilled in thinking creatively, generating ideas, and identifying alternative ways of accomplishing any given activity. Resourceful women are imaginative and can visualize how to achieve the seemingly impossible. Determination enables them to stay the course and emerge victorious.

Since resourcefulness is a mind-set, the resourceful woman must not always look to her own imagination for help. She would always be wise to tap into the resources available through other resourceful men and women in her circle of interaction.

Part 2

COUNTERPRODUCTIVE TENDENCIES TO LET GO

As we continue to embrace and manage the God-given traits that help us succeed in our leadership roles, we must become equally diligent in realizing when we are engaging in self-sabotage. Let's face it; we can unwittingly be our own worst enemy. In this section, we will look at the traits, tendencies, and mind-sets that thwart our progress. I'm going to ask you to be honest in owning them and then be willing to use the doable strategies I'll propose to let them go.

LACKING CONFIDENCE

No one can make you feel inferior without your consent.

—Eleanor Roosevelt, first lady of the United States
(March 4, 1933–April 12, 1945)

On April 17, 2018, Captain Tammie Jo Shults performed an emergency landing of a crippled Southwest Airlines 737 twin-engine jet with competence and extraordinary calm after an engine exploded and its shrapnel went through the window, fatally wounding a passenger. The lives of the remaining 148 people on board flight 1380 from New York to Dallas were spared due to Shults's quick thinking. She was well prepared for the job. Captain Shults had been one of the first female fighter pilots in the US Navy. According to a former classmate, when Shults enlisted in the Navy, she encountered "a lot of resistance because of her gender. She knew she had to work harder than everyone else…She did it for herself and all women fighting for a chance."[1] Shults had long been an advocate for diversity in the workforce and encouraged women to break through in male-dominated fields. In safely landing the plane, Captain Shults displayed the kind of confidence usually ascribed to a man. We learn from her book, *Nerves of Steel,* that the source of her assurance was her abiding faith in God. Not every woman walks in that kind of confidence. In this chapter, we will discuss how you too can rise to new levels of assurance.

When I graduated as valedictorian of my predominantly white high school class in 1968, some people told me I had three strikes against me as I prepared to face the world: I am a woman. I am black. I am a dark-skinned black woman. Yikes! Three strikes. In baseball parlance, that meant that I'd already struck out before I had my turn at bat! Fortunately, I learned early on not to accept the conclusions that other people make about my potential—even when put forth by well-meaning church leaders, experts, or researchers based on their own "findings." Since then, I've gone on to overcome numerous personal and professional adversities, which I'm sharing throughout this book. My secret? I have a core belief that informs my attitude and my actions. It is vastly different from the secular wisdom of our day. *I believe I am connected to the all-powerful (omnipotent), all-knowing (omniscient), and always-present (omnipresent) God who created the universe.* By embracing this truth, I have come to believe that I am never inadequate for any task or assignment.

A deeper look at the origin of the word *confidence* explains my mind-set. The prefix *con* means *with* and the root word *fid* means trust. When combined with *self*, self-confidence means "with trust in self." The self relies on what it has learned or experienced. Life is too uncertain to park our faith on such a shaky foundation. Besides, Proverbs 28:26 (NIV) boldly declares, "Those who trust in themselves are fools." Thus I am not on a mission to increase my self-confidence, since the pursuit of it is spiritually foolish and practically exasperating. Such efforts also fly in face of 2 Corinthians 3:5 (KJV): "Not that we are sufficient of ourselves to think of anything as being from ourselves, but our sufficiency *is* from God."

Am I suggesting that we abandon all personal development efforts and passively expect God to do everything? Absolutely not. We partner with him by doing our part in the natural realm (getting educated, taking risks, networking effectively, etc.), while he supernaturally gives us favor with others, wisdom, and revelation regarding actions to take that will cause everything to work together for our good when we are trusting him. I call this walking in supreme confidence. This kind of confidence can produce results beyond our wildest imagination and abilities.

Competence Versus Confidence

Entrenched stereotypes, social customs, and unconscious bias have led many people to believe that leadership is a man's domain—especially in business. It appears that many women have also bought into this thinking. Over the years, I've met women with stellar qualifications who lacked the confidence to lead. It is not in our best interest as women to spend our time or energy trying to convince a male-dominated society to change its mind-set. Our best strategy is to bring our *A*-game to the table along with a positive attitude and to lead with care, concern, and confidence. We must let go of any anger or chips on our shoulders about how others *should* think about women in power. To refuse to do so will only impede our progress. Our time would be better spent overcoming our lack of confidence.

Award-winning filmmaker Ava DuVernay's take on competence and confidence is refreshing and worth emulating:

Me: Ava, I heard a popular talk show host say that she had interviewed tens of thousands of people, and that inadequacy was a common thread they all shared. In observing you, it seems that confidence is your calling card. How is it that you have developed such confidence, other than being competent, of course?

Ava: My confidence comes from knowing that I don't know everything. Many people walk into a room and put on airs as if they know everything. They try to project power or appear to be an expert at something. I walk in with no problem saying, "I don't know the answer to that. Let's find out together," or, "What do you think about that?" "Hmmm, I'm not sure about that; let me think about it some more." None of those things is diminishing. They actually give you power. No one knows everything. There is a lack of confidence embedded in pretending. But if you don't know, you just don't know. Acknowledging it allows you to be confident in what you don't know. This opens you up to new ideas and new ways of being.

Why Confidence Is Crucial

It is important for a woman to exhibit confidence, since it is *not* one of the stereotypical gender-based expectations for female leadership. In other words, men are assumed to be confident. However, from my four decades of corporate experience, to be perceived as an effective leader a woman must be careful to display confidence in conjunction with her inherent leadership traits, such as being communicative, collaborative, caring, and so forth. Without these traits, she risks being viewed as cocky or arrogant. "Hey, that's not fair," you may be shouting. My goal here is not to get stuck on what "should" be but to make you aware of the subtle pitfalls that often cause a woman to be negatively perceived or evaluated.

It is important for a woman to exhibit confidence, since it is *not* one of the stereotypical gender-based expectations for female leadership.

When you walk in divine assurance, you can expect it to yield these benefits:

- *Confidence inspires and motives others.* People may admire your competence, but it will be your confidence that will inspire your staff or followers to support you. They believe that you will succeed because of who you are. The book of Judges recounts the story of Deborah, the only female judge of the Israelites before they were ruled by kings. Deborah was a prophetess and obviously known to have a close connection to God. When she challenged Barak, the army general, to conscript a 10,000-man army to attack the well-supplied army of their oppressor, he replied, "I will go, but only if you go with me."[2] She went with him, and they prevailed against the enemy as she had prophesied. Barak had no ego on display when he declared his assurance of victory simply because of Deborah's presence.

- *Confidence engenders risk-taking.* One of the fundamentals of investing is "low risk, low reward; high risk, high reward." A woman who is comfortable taking a risk on an unproven process, product, or other unknown positions her organization or department for high rewards. No one is applauded for maintaining the status quo.

   Here is what Dr. Aimee V. Sanchez, clinical neuropsychologist, leadership coach, and author of *Disrupt the Status Quo: Living and Leading from Your Success Zone*, had to say when I queried her about risk-taking:

   > Risk-taking is part of my DNA. I have always been inquisitive, thus, I tend to thrive when I color outside the lines. I see myself as a calculated risk-taker. But I wouldn't say that I always ignore the potential downside of risks. If a decision will impact others in a critical way, I solicit feedback before moving forward. Sometimes that feedback compels me even more to advocate for taking the risk. Some of my peers have expressed that I'm sometimes too willing to embrace change. The complexity of my style of leadership allows me to maintain balance and structure while also asking "What if?" This style of leadership has positioned me for unique professional opportunities and allowed me to remain agile in my thought processes, allowed me to lead high performing teams, and provided me with a sense of freedom both personally and professionally because I chose to lean into the fear.

- *Confidence minimizes stress.* Whenever you are able to relieve performance anxiety, you put yourself in a position of strength. Your confidence need not always come from your winning history. Sometimes, it's a matter of reminding yourself that the outcome does not depend on you but on your ever-present Heavenly Father.

How to Become Supremely Confident

Becoming a woman who walks in a high level of confidence takes time and effort—and trial and error. Don't shy away from the process. Here are some strategies that can help you on your journey:

1. *Acknowledge and appreciate your God-given strengths.* It really is okay to honor what you bring to the table and to realize how it adds value to your organization and your fellow workers.

2. *Shift your reliance from your strengths to God's unlimited power and presence.* This mind-set is key. Since confidence means "with trust," why begin any endeavor relying on self-confidence?

3. *Let your self-talk and prayers reflect and reinforce your faith.* "God, my eyes are on you to bring this assignment to a successful end. I know that you can do exceedingly above all that I could ask or think, so help me hear and heed your voice every step of the way."

4. *Address practical hindrances to your confidence.* Here is where you may not have 20/20 vision on yourself and may need to hire the services of an image consultant or other professional—or just listen to a trusted, stylish friend. Is your smile distracting due to needed dental work? Making the investment to fix the problem will be money well spent. You may also need to upgrade your wardrobe or hairdo to reflect current styles and more flattering colors for your skin tone. Feeling good about your appearance is a great confidence booster. What about your energy level? Do

you project enthusiasm and passion for your career? If you are lethargic for reasons within your control, talk to your doctor and develop a plan to increase your vitality.

5. *Proactively engage your fears.* No, not all at once. Confidence must be developed over time. Select one fear that may be holding you back and run toward it. Think of practical steps you can take now to overcome it. Fearful of public speaking? I dare you to post a 60-second Facebook video or volunteer to make an announcement or lead a discussion group. Lean into the idea of being uncomfortable. See it as a requirement for growth. Amazingly, when you overcome one fear, it emboldens you to conquer others. As you gain more influence, you may indeed become the fish in the proverbial fishbowl. Consider it an opportunity to display to the world the inherent traits God has given you and most women that make them dynamic leaders.

6. *Take back your power from "they."* "They" are the nameless people that you have unwittingly given control over your decision-making and pursuits. They cause you to live in constant anxiety, a puppet of their opinions. You may even manage your finances unwisely so that they will regard you more highly because of your trappings of success. If they don't like or approve of you, you label yourself a failure. You will not achieve your God-given destiny if you continue to focus on what they say or think. When they offer their unsolicited opinions, graciously respond, "Thank you for your input. God and I are working it out." Also, consider that sometimes, they may not exist in reality but rather are your imaginary critics born out of your own insecurity. Ignore them!

7. *Guard against pride.* Caution! It will be important to monitor your mind-set as you ease into becoming more confident. It can be tempting, if you are not careful, to

go from being insecure to confident to cocky. If you find yourself being filled with pride over your newfound confidence, try these strategies:

1. Remember that whatever you have achieved or overcome, you have done so by the grace (divine enablement and favor) of God—and that he has a history of toppling those who walk in pride.

2. Be genuinely interested in others. Ask sincere questions about their projects, goals, and aspirations. Listen to their responses and make encouraging comments.

3. Do not boast about your achievements or the influential people in your network. Doing so is a sign of insecurity, a sure indication of the source of your self-worth.

When you embrace the powerful concept of walking in supreme confidence, you show up differently for life's challenges. You stop focusing on your perceived inadequacies or disadvantages or the advantages of your competitors. Your attitude and responses will begin to reflect an expectation of God. You will take risks, speak up, and even engage a task for which you have neither the experience nor knowledge to succeed. Most of all, you will experience the peace of knowing you are empowered by an all-powerful, all-knowing, and always-present Supreme Being who wants you to win—to be more than a conqueror. Sisters, decide now to put away the anxiety, the self-doubt, and the limited thinking and to walk in supreme confidence.

14

PURSUING PERFECTION

*Perfectionism is a mind-set of self-defeating thoughts
and behaviors aimed at reaching unrealistic goals.*

—Deborah Smith Pegues

So what that you'd like everything to be "just right"? Isn't perfectionism an admirable and socially applauded trait? Why, some people wear it like a badge of honor. It parades itself as a virtue, which is why it is the most cited trait in job interviews. However, we must challenge this myth that it is something positive. It is nothing more than a sophisticated version of fear. On the surface, it earns us praise for having high standards and working hard. Underneath, it gives us a false sense of control and worth.

The Root of Perfectionism

I once wore perfectionism like a badge of honor...until I recognized the detrimental effect it was having on the staff that I managed. I further realized that at the root of my quest for error-free reports and outcomes was the fear that the mistakes the staff made would cause others to think that I was personally incompetent. I held a historically male role and the buck stopped with me. My department was responsible for accurately budgeting, recording, and reporting all financial transactions and for issuing quarterly and annual charitable contribution statements to more than 23,000 donors. Too many errors could put the credibility and integrity of the high-profile organization at risk. The staff knew that I had high standards and that I did not tolerate poor performance; therefore, they felt that each mistake brought them closer to a reprimand and even being fired.

After a series of staff mess-ups, I was at my wit's end. I had documented procedures, maintained an open-door policy for real-time response to their questions, and had done all that I knew to ensure an efficient operation. I earnestly prayed for a breakthrough. I decided to adopt a new mind-set and a new strategy for the situation. I called a staff meeting and set everyone free from the perfection prison. I set a reasonable error rate for incorrect contribution statements and asked the staff to note ways that we could avoid repeating the same mistakes in the future. I even shared with them several instances in which I had made mistakes. A marvelous thing happened. Their anxiety levels dropped and morale soared. We became a real family—right at work. The finger-pointing stopped because team solutions became more important than placing blame. In our staff meetings, we even started to find humor in some of the errors—which, by the way, decreased significantly!

Pursuing perfection is futile. Famed psychologist Dr. David Viscott explained how it can turn you into a control freak:

> A controlling adult's wish to be perfect stems from the childhood wish to be blameless. Since real growth means embracing your faults and examining your weaknesses, controlling people run the greatest risk of becoming rigid and failing because of their insistence on always being right. They need to feel they are beyond criticism so that no one will have a good reason for withholding what they need or rejecting them. They believe they need to be perfect just to be safe, so admitting even small imperfections makes them uneasy and self-doubting. If they can be imperfect in one way, they reason, they could be imperfect in others. Since being imperfect is a fact of life, acknowledging themselves honestly is a continual threat to their self-esteem. Even slight criticisms compel them to refute others' logic and testimony.[1]

**A controlling adult's wish to be perfect stems
from the childhood wish to be blameless.**

Today, many people believe that being a perfectionist is desirable and necessary for success. The quest for perfection is one of the biggest obstacles many women face as leaders. Because women often must work harder to get a seat at the table among their male counterparts, they are more likely than men to be perfectionists. This can lead to risk avoidance and low confidence.

A wise person coined the phrase "Done is better than perfect." The phrase is popular because it's the truth. Consider this scenario. Suppose you desire to write three blogs a week or five pages per day or you want to exercise five days a week. Often, when perfectionists realize that their goal is not possible, they default to the mind-set, "Why even bother at all." Rather than doing what they can—such as writing one blog a week, writing one page a day, or exercising three days a week—they simply do nothing. It sounds illogical, but this is the reality for many perfectionists.

You would think that the pursuit of perfection would make one confident, but it has the opposite effect—it lowers your self-confidence rather than raises it. Thus it is important to set realistic expectations. Women must let go of their all-or-nothing attitudes.

Signs of Perfectionism

Are you ready to admit that you are a perfectionist, or are you still clinging to the label of being a high achiever? There is a difference. High achievers are dedicated and determined to accomplish the goals they have set. Their motivation comes from within. They are not trying to accomplish something just to make themselves look good to others or to avoid looking bad. Their motivation is personal gratification. They work hard to complete a project, and when it's done, they feel good. It may not be perfect, but it is good enough to serve its purpose well. On the other hand, perfectionists are motivated by the need to avoid failure. Their motivation is externally driven. They work hard to complete a project and then obsess that perhaps they should do something to make it even better. Studies show that true perfectionists aren't really trying to be perfect. They are avoiding not being good enough. This behavior can lead to depression, eating disorders, anxiety, and, in a worst-case scenario, suicide. Below is a brief list of some of the signs that behavioral experts generally agree are an indication that you are a perfectionist:

1. *You don't allow yourself to make mistakes.* The average person realizes that everyone is human and thus prone to mistakes. Perfectionists rarely view mistakes as an opportunity for growth and improvement. In extreme cases, their mistakes can lead them to paralyzing inaction.

2. *You avoid situations in which you might fail.* You play it safe and stick with what you know rather than branching out and taking on new challenges. You have trouble moving beyond your comfort zone because you might fail if you take on the unknown.

3. *You have difficulty delegating.* You hold onto the belief that "if you want it done right, you have to do it yourself." In so doing, you micromanage and set yourself up for burnout. Plus, you deprive your staff of the opportunity to develop their skills.

4. *Despite striving for perfection, you don't feel perfect.* Even after achieving the goals you set for yourself, such as getting a promotion or completing a challenging project, you don't feel perfect. You obsess that you could have done things even better. You are always searching for the next thing that will make you feel good enough.

5. *You are often late in completing projects.* This seems counter-intuitive. After all, if a person wants to be perfect, wouldn't they turn everything in early? However, the constant

thought of messing up the project hampers productivity and increases the tendency to procrastinate.

Avoiding the Trap

In our striving for excellence, we must be motivated by passion rather than fear of failure. Perfectionism is often an ingrained behavior; therefore, it will take intentional effort to avoid falling into its trap. But this can be done with self-awareness and dedication and keeping an eye on the following:

- *Procrastination.* People procrastinate for a variety of reasons, but for perfectionists, this is a red flag that must be acknowledged and overcome. Perfectionism not only stops people from completing a task; it often stops people from beginning a task. If you are procrastinating, you are either worried about what someone else will think or worried about whether you can adequately perform the job—that it won't be perfect.

- *Wallowing.* Sometimes one mistake will cause a perfectionist to wallow in it rather than recover and get back on track. For example, suppose that you are on a diet, a stressful situation arises, and you decided to find refuge in a piece of cake. You believe that, since you have already messed up, you might as well have another, or you go off your diet and binge for the rest of the day rather than just starting over and recommitting to making a better choice next time.

- *Unrealistic expectations.* Because perfectionists tend to aim high, they sometimes set unrealistic expectations for themselves. Many high-achieving women will impose on themselves the role of an "official representative" for all women or on behalf of an entire ethnic group. They feel the pressure of trying to walk a narrow line of perfection in order to guard against perpetuating a negative stereotype, such as "women are too emotional" or "all black women are angry." I was heartened by the balanced, emotionally healthy approach to this issue taken by Hollywood filmmaker Ava DuVernay. With Disney's movie *A Wrinkle in Time*, she became the first black female director whose movie grossed more than $100 million at the domestic box office. When I interviewed her, I asked her to weigh in on this mind-set.

> *Me:*   Ava, as is often the case with many high-achieving minorities, especially women, they feel that they must "represent" their group well and do everything possible to maintain an admirable image. Do you feel that you carry the burden of the black race, that you are always representing African Americans, and that whatever you do is a reflection on or an accolade for the entire race?

> *Ava:*   I do carry that, but not as a burden. I carry it as an honor. I carry my ancestors, my family, my community, and the different rooms of myself. In my industry, where I am one of the few who are doing this, it doesn't feel heavy but is truly an honor for me.

- *Enoughness.* Enoughness is the concept that at a certain point in any given project or endeavor, it is good enough. Perfectionists often think nothing is ever good enough, so they fail before they begin. If you are that person, combat this tendency by determining what will be "enough" for you before you start a task. When you reach that benchmark, congratulate yourself and then consider it done.

Indeed, striving for perfection comes at a great cost, making it more difficult to be satisfied with your work and with yourself. You must remember that your work does not determine your worth.

Perfectionism causes you to be less willing to experiment with new things and get out of your comfort zone. It causes you to downplay accomplishments and shoot down compliments. As Leo Tolstoy said, "If you look for perfection, you'll never be content."

Continue to have high standards, but don't let it spiral out of control. You simply need to develop new thought patterns about yourself and your accomplishments. Take risks and give yourself permission to make mistakes. When you are brave enough to try new things, you embrace a more creative, innovative, confident you. This improves your leadership skills and makes you more relatable to those you lead. So be kind to yourself, knowing that there is not one perfect human on planet Earth—and that failure is not fatal.

15

DISFAVORING OTHER WOMEN

A candle loses nothing when it lights another candle.

—Italian proverb

Scarcity of an item can cause people to compete to obtain a share of it or to fight to hang onto it. Welcome to the relational dynamics of organizations or groups where women leaders are rare. Support from other women will often be nonexistent, and competition can be fierce and sometimes downright mean.

While I have indeed encountered an occasional lack of support from other women, most that I've interacted with have been remarkable in their support. I offer high praise and gratitude for my friends and fellow inspirational speakers Deborah Cobrae, Kathleen Cooke, Cindy Fahy, P. Bunny Wilson, Terri McFaddin-Solomon, Dr. Saundra Dalton Smith, and others who have graciously shared their influence and wisdom and proactively opened doors on my behalf in significant venues. These women of various ethnic backgrounds have an abundance mind-set and believe there are enough blessings for us all to share. They have refused to adopt the scarcity belief there is only one "speaking pie" out there and if they share theirs with me, there will be fewer opportunities for them. I'm equally grateful for numerous friends for their faithful prayers, encouraging text messages, marketing expertise, traveling companionship, and back-of-the-room sales assistance at various engagements. But what do you do when this kind of support is absent? And how can you model such support so that aspiring leaders and others know what it looks like?

Letting Go of the Queen Bee Syndrome

Have you had the distinction of being the first or only woman ever to serve in a certain position? It can be a heady feeling atop that pedestal. It can also be tempting to try to secure your place by making sure no other woman gets near it. Enter the "queen bee." In the world of bees, only one queen lives in each hive. "She is the only female with fully developed ovaries," so she lays all the eggs. "In general, queen bees use their stingers only to kill rival queens that may emerge or be introduced in the hive."[1]

In the world of leadership, the queen bee is the woman who has achieved an exalted position but withholds support from other women desiring to advance through the ranks. According to historians and biographers, Margaret Thatcher (aka "The Iron Lady") was a queen bee personified. She was the first woman elected to lead a major Western power. She was the longest-serving British prime minister in 150 years. She was "the most dominant and the most divisive force in British politics in the second half of the twentieth century."[2] She was "famous for rarely promoting other women." She was "the only woman in the room and didn't want any competition."[3]

I've achieved several "first woman" and "first black" distinctions over the course of my professional career. My spiritual mentors taught me early on that there was a divine purpose for the platform that the distinctions afforded me and that if I used it for "self-glory," I would incur God's wrath. They put the fear in me. To reinforce their admonition, I frequently read the story in Daniel 4 about King Nebuchadnezzar, who bragged about his conquests. Consequently, God stripped him of his sanity for seven years and banished him to the fields to live like an animal. Afterward, God showed him mercy and restored his mind and his kingdom. The humbled king didn't waste any time acknowledging that God is in control of the affairs of mankind. Having read his story, I have been scared stiff of ever behaving like a queen bee.

Women of faith should be the prime examples when it comes to supporting other women, for we embrace the Bible, which assures us that "exaltation comes neither from the east nor from the west nor from the south. But God is the Judge: He puts down one, and exalts another."[4] I'm always saddened when I hear of a leading woman of faith disfavoring another, for it is a sign that she believes she must forge her way apart from God.

Ladies, let's make it a habit of praising other women and building them up. When you hear or observe that your female peers have done a great job, be quick to give them credit—especially where it counts: to their bosses or followers. Don't fret that you may be deflecting the light from yourself. God sees your accomplishments and will exalt you in due season. Besides, your actions will speak loudly to others that you are a secure team player with an abundance mentality and with enough confidence to praise another.

One of the best examples of one woman praising another is found in the story of Deborah (Judges 4). She was a prophetess, counselor, and the only female judge of Israel. When she charged Barak, captain of the northern kingdom's army, to launch an attack against King Jabin, Israel's well-equipped, longtime oppressor, he insisted that she go into battle with him. She consented but prophesied that the victory over Sisera, the commander of Jabin's army, would be at the hands of a woman. Sure enough, the Israelites prevailed in the battle. Sisera, seeing his army totally annihilated, fled on foot. Jael, the wife of a King Jabin supporter but a sympathizer of Israel, welcomed the exhausted warrior into her tent. She gave him milk and made him comfortable. When he fell into a deep sleep, she snuck up on him, hammered a tent peg into his head, and killed him. Later, Deborah and Barak sang a song (*The Song of Deborah*) of the battle, and in the song, they honored Jael:

> Most blessed among women is Jael,
> The wife of Heber the Kenite;
> Blessed is she among women in tents.
> He asked for water, she gave milk;
> She brought out cream in a lordly bowl.
> She stretched her hand to the tent peg,

Her right hand to the workmen's hammer;
She pounded Sisera, she pierced his head,
She split and struck through his temple.
At her feet he sank, he fell, he lay still;
At her feet he sank, he fell;
Where he sank, there he fell dead.[5]

Deborah did not conduct herself as a queen bee. She applauded Jael and memorialized her bravery for all eternity. When was the last time that you sang another woman's praise?

Unsupportive Female Subordinates

Sometimes your support of other women may not be reciprocated. Such was the case with "Donna," who worked for a small investment firm in the mid-1980s. The staff consisted of four executives (three males and Donna as the investment analyst / portfolio director), and "Sheri," their administrative assistant. Sheri faithfully brought the men their coffee each morning like clockwork. Not being a coffee drinker, Donna requested her to fill her small ice bucket each day for chilling her water. To her disappointment, Donna had to remind Sheri almost every single day to bring the ice from the conveniently located dispenser. She was extremely frustrated by Sheri's reluctance to accommodate her request. After all, she had known her for several years, had recommended her for the job, and had continually mentored and supported her professional growth and development. Sensing a bit of a negative attitude, Donna confronted her.

Donna: Sheri, I notice that I must remind you each day to get my ice. Is there a problem?

Sheri: (after a moment of contemplation followed by a deep sigh) "I…I don't know…I guess it just feels funny serving a woman. Yeah, I think that's what it is. I've never had to serve a woman."

Donna was surprised by Sheri's candid admission. She felt she deserved equal or even greater support from Sheri. Unlike the guys, she had demonstrated a personal interest in Sheri's professional development. Sheri's bias toward "serving a woman" cut to Donna's core. She struggled inwardly on how to recast their seemingly one-sided relationship going forward. She knew that Sheri hadn't had much exposure to women in leadership in the business world; plus, they had a hoard of mutual friends in their social network outside of the office. The tension between the two of them would have made it uncomfortable for everybody. Although Sheri's attitude had dampened Donna's motivation to continue to invest personal time in helping her maximize her potential, Donna decided to help her work through her now-conscious bias and naïveté regarding office politics. Sheri would surely encounter a similar situation as she advanced in her career. Donna and Sheri have remained friends to this day. And just for the record, Donna did not relieve her of the duty of getting the ice!

Similar scenarios continue to be played out in organizations where a female subordinate is stuck in her thinking that an executive woman is not deserving of treatment equal to that afforded a male executive. *After all*, some surmise, *all women are equal; women serve men only.* Ladies, if you aspire to be a leader, don't be that person. Be honest with yourself about your "why" for being unsupportive, remember the Golden Rule, and do the right thing whether you feel like it or not. Don't assume your female boss has the emotional intelligence or spiritual maturity to look beyond your unwise action. She just may hold a grudge against you and begin to subtly sabotage future opportunities.

Now, if you happen to be the leader who is discriminated against, confront the situation with grace, seek to help the perpetrator understand its root cause, and reiterate your expectations.

Resisting the "Leveling Syndrome"

Many women, feeling "less than" when comparing their efforts to another woman's success in an endeavor, will often engage in what I call the "leveling syndrome." They make statements or assertions designed to minimize another woman's accomplishment or to elevate their own perceived "one-down" status. For example, say Ellen has written 20 books that have sold millions of copies. Her colleague Lora has been in the process of writing a book for several years but, for various reasons, she has not finished it. Feeling somewhat like a failure, Lora says to Ellen, "Wow, Joyce Meyer has written more than 50 books and is still going strong. What a writing machine!" What Lora is really thinking is "I'm feeling inferior to you; therefore, I'll add someone to the equation who outshines you, to bring you down a notch, and to cause you to feel inferior also. There, I've leveled the playing field." Ladies, do not be a Lora. *Stop thinking that all women must maintain equal status professionally or be "leveled" or rejected.* Learn how to *act* happy for those who excel, even if you do not feel such goodwill. This is not being hypocritical; you are teaching yourself a new way—God's way—to respond to others' blessings. I often say that *feelings follow actions*, so get busy congratulating achievers and praising their works to others, even when they are not around. Going against your natural tendency in this way will forge a new and more pleasant attitude.

Slaying the Green-Eyed Monster

Unlike jealousy, which is rooted in the *fear* of being displaced, envy is born out of *discontentment* with one's situation. It shows up in leadership when a colleague or friend gets a promotion, accolades, or an advantage that you desire and deserve. If you fall into the envy trap, it is unlikely that you will seek help in getting out of it. Envy is probably one of the most unconfessed or denied character flaws. Why, have you ever heard someone say, "Pray for me. I'm harboring ill will toward Jane because she has gotten what I want"?

> Unlike jealousy, which is rooted in the *fear* of being displaced, envy is born out of *discontentment* with one's situation.

Emotionally savvy women are wise to recognize envy as a sign to reevaluate their efforts and priorities. The following introspective questions will help you start to get to the root of your envy and get on the path to a better mind-set and outcome:

- "What practical steps do I need to take next in order to move my objectives forward?"
- "What price will I have to pay to achieve my objective?"
- "Am I willing and ready now to pay that price?"
- "Is it worth it spiritually, relationally, physically, emotionally, or financially to do so?"

I've asked myself these questions many a time when envy has reared its head. And I've seen many ambitious, go-getter women relegate their husbands and family to a secondary priority in order to reach the pinnacle of their careers. I've read about their success in the media—sometimes with a tinge of envy—before recalling the hard choices I've made over the years to forgo certain opportunities in order to balance my career and my now four-decade, happy marriage. My choices were not always easy, but they were best for me and I have no regrets.

Harnessing the Power of Unity

Many successful women leaders are still reluctant to advocate for other women, choosing rather to ignore or even disadvantage them. Ambitious peers gossip, say harsh words, and emotionally bully others. Ladies, we are better than that. We already know that unity is a place of power. We have seen the impact when women have banded together: the Me Too movement toppled high-level perpetrators, elections were swung, gender quotas are being established in male-dominated industries, pay gap inequities are being addressed, and empowerment measures are abounding worldwide. We must always remember that lighting our sister's candle will not extinguish ours. Let's do our part to show one another that we are committed to our equality. We may not embrace the same political or other beliefs, but the quest for cultural change requires courage to speak out and to confront discrimination and disadvantages whenever we have the opportunity. Let's not criticize those who are on the frontlines of change but rather pray that they will promote God-honoring objectives.

I'm making every effort to show my appreciation for those who have supported me by paying it forward and sharing information and resources with aspiring leaders across generations and cultures. As a woman of faith, I take comfort in knowing that no one can thwart God's purpose for my life. This truth frees me to be an enthusiastic cheerleader for other women and the best possible team player, since I am not competing against anyone for my divine destiny. It is already assured.

CHRONIC MULTITASKING

*Better to have one handful with quietness than two
handfuls with hard work and chasing the wind.*

Ecclesiastes 4:6

Most female baby boomers remember the Enjoli perfume commercial that painted the picture of a woman who could do it all—bring home the bacon, take care of the house, and please her man—all while wearing high heels, a suit, and never breaking a sweat. And why was she able to do all this? Her answer: "Because I'm a woman!"[1]

Women and Multitasking: The Deadly Duo

The Enjoli perfume commercial promoted a competent, beautiful, smart, capable woman—a superwoman. And this view of a woman has not changed much over the years. We are still known to be multitaskers, getting it all done seemingly efficiently. On the other hand, men are viewed as having one-track minds, unable to focus on more than one thing at a time. Even though a University of Pennsylvania study showed that there are more neural connections between the left and right side of women's brains than men's, it did not conclude that women are wired for multitasking; we simply practice it more often because we carry a higher variety of responsibilities on the domestic and professional front.

The Cost of Multitasking

Multitasking is often seen as a positive act. We applaud ourselves and others for getting several things done at once. Many people list multitasking on their resumes as a skill. However, it is a myth. And, because of this myth, we have convinced ourselves we are getting things done when, in reality, our productivity plummets as much as 40 percent.[2] Consider these downsides of multitasking:

Multitasking creates the illusion of productivity, but it is the opposite. Every time we quickly switch from one project to another, our brain must take time to readjust and reorient itself to the new task.

Multitasking creates the illusion of
productivity, but it is the opposite.

Frequent multitasking is detrimental to your memory. Memory loss and absentmindedness are very common among those who multitask regularly. Our brain is not designed to handle too many tasks at the same time. Also, when you are juggling between two different activities, you are not paying proper attention to either one of them. So whatever you are doing or learning, you will not be able to recollect it properly later. Short-term memory loss is a regular phenomenon but beware: multitasking can even damage your permanent memory.

Multitasking kills your creativity. While multitasking, your attention switches from one problem to another. You may be able to work on many tasks at one time, but you will really struggle in those that require some serious problem-solving. This is because your brain becomes so accustomed to shifting tasks that it is no longer able to concentrate on one thing with full concentration. So do not make it a habit of checking emails while working on a tough problem. You may take a break, reply to your chats, and then resume working again.[3]

Multitasking does not exist. Dave Crenshaw, author of *The Myth of Multitasking: How Doing It All Gets Nothing Done*, puts forth the idea that there is no such thing as multitasking. There are only *switchtasking* and *background tasking*. Switchtasking is attempting to do multiple tasks at the same time. Rather than truly doing more than one task at once, we are merely quickly switching between tasks. Background tasking is performing a primary task while performing a less significant task in the background—for example, exercising while listening to music. Background tasking may improve productivity, while switchtasking results in a decrease in productivity.

Switchtasking has a negative impact on three primary areas: time, quality, and stress. It results in each task taking longer than if you had simply focused on one at a time, and the quality of the work will decrease as well. Finally, multitasking increases, not decreases, stress. Switchtasking comes at a cost, and the dividends aren't worth what you have to pay. Dave offers an interesting exercise on his website (https://davecrenshaw.com/myth-of-multitasking-exercise/) to help you see how efficient you are at multitasking.[4]

A Time Management Issue

Multitasking is ultimately a time management problem. Think about it. If you felt you had enough time to get things done, you wouldn't try to do them all at once. Of course, sometimes multitasking is unavoidable. For example, you may have a job where you must take phone calls and type information at the same time. But for everyone else, switchtasking should be avoided as much as possible. The following are some steps to help you better manage your time:

- *Manage interruptions.* Every time you experience an interruption, ask yourself what you can do to minimize the chance of it happening again.

- *Reduce your gathering points.* Gathering points are those places where we typically "store" unresolved issues. We may use a notebook, a calendar, sticky notes, an app, a chalkboard, and so on. The idea is to limit yourself to no more than six of these gathering points to be more efficient and productive.

- *Use a calendar instead of a to-do list.* To-do lists can be beneficial, but they often lack a timeline for completing a task. Therefore, a calendar is a better tool for recording to-do items.

- *Learn to say no more often.* Any time you say yes to something, you are saying no to something else. Saying no will allow you to get more of the things you need done.

- *Stop using your email in-box as a storage place.* You should take care of each item one at a time and try to completely clear your in-box at least once a week. Either delete items or store them in a more permanent folder. (At the time of this writing, I have more than 65,000 unread emails; please follow my advice but not my example.)

- *Build a buffer into your schedule.* Building in a buffer means that you don't schedule tasks for every minute of every day. It means building in some downtime so that if something comes up, you don't feel rushed and stressed. For example, if you typically schedule multiple meetings a day, don't schedule them for an hour each starting at 1 p.m., 2 p.m., 3 p.m., and so on. Instead, schedule meetings for 50 minutes to allow for a 10-minute buffer between meetings to take a breather and gather your thoughts.

- *Commit to your calendar.* Don't schedule something in your calendar and then fail to follow through unless there is a true emergency. Often, we skip important tasks due to our emotions (depression, anxiety, etc.), but it's best to focus on the emotion you will feel once the task is complete rather than on how you feel (or don't feel) at the moment.[5]

Putting an End to Multitasking

At best, multitasking will waste your time, encourage more mistakes, and stress you out unnecessarily, to name a few outcomes. At worst, it could cost someone their life. Consider the story of a woman who was doing nothing more than driving and talking on her phone. She wasn't texting or scrolling on Facebook, just talking. However, she was distracted enough that she ran a red light and hit a car, killing a 12-year-old boy.[6] This is an extreme example, but it points out how juggling even seemingly small tasks can hamper our focus and take our attention away from that which is most important.

When we multitask, we are teaching ourselves *not* to focus, and that can be a dangerous thing indeed. Try these tips to break the chronic multitasking cycle.

1. *Focus more and work less.* When you work fewer hours, it forces you to become more efficient at the work you do. Give yourself short deadlines to help you focus and complete the project without interruption. You will be less likely to answer an unimportant call if you only have 30 minutes to complete a presentation.

2. *Eliminate distractions.* While we can't eliminate every single distraction from our lives, we do have a fair amount of control. This will look different for each person, depending on your personality and temperament. For example, some may have to put their phone across the room until they finish a project. Others may only have to turn off the sound.

3. *Prioritize your to-do list.* Many of us, when confronted with our to-do list, choose the easiest and most unimportant things first. By the time we get around to the things that really needed to get done, we're suddenly out of time and need to multitask to complete them. Start by numbering your items in the order of importance and systematically work through each one until you finish.

4. *Work in timed intervals.* Since I'm convinced that I function better under pressure, here's an effective hack I use to force myself to complete or make headway on a project. I set the alarm on my watch for a specific time period (ranging from 10 to 30 minutes) and only work on a certain task for that period. Since it's better on my back to take frequent breaks, when the alarm sounds, I'll stand up and stretch or perform 100 jumps on my deskside trampoline. You can adapt this technique to suit your task, personality, or environment and allow for shorter or longer intervals. The key is to take the breaks. You will be able to better focus on the project because you know you have a break coming up soon.

5. *Block out time-wasting websites.* The scenario is common— you do a little work and then go check Facebook. Do some more work and decide to go pay a bill online. Then you remember that item you wanted to purchase from Amazon. Before you know it, you've spent several hours of your workday on things other than work. There are many applications that allow you to block your browser or certain websites. They include StayFocusd,[7] FocusMe,[8] and OffTime.[9]

Multitasking robs you of valuable time, rather than giving you more of it. What would you do with several extra hours a month? Get more sleep? Spend more time with family? Giving up multitasking can give you back these crucial hours and allow you to spend more time doing things you enjoy.

DOWNPLAYING SKILLS AND ACCOMPLISHMENTS

*But whatever I am now, it is all because God
poured out his special favor on me—and not
without results. For I have worked harder than
any of the other apostles; yet it was not I but God
who was working through me by his grace.*

1 Corinthians 15:10

From an early age, girls don't appreciate other girls who seem too sure of themselves or who appear to be superior to others. Little girls who have learned this lesson often carry it over into adulthood and are reluctant to display their excellence to other women. Most women avoid mentioning their accomplishments, choosing rather to understate them. A Japanese quote sums this ideology up well, "A nail that sticks up gets hammered down." Even the Bible admonishes, "Let someone else praise you, not your own mouth."[1] But there is a difference between *acknowledging* an achievement and *praising* yourself for it.

Catching Yourself in Action

Many women who are more successful than their friends feel guilty about this imbalance and want to protect the feelings of others and protect themselves from alienation and rejection. Thus they try to avoid appearing more knowledgeable or successful. In conversations with other women, there is often an unspoken social ritual taking place in which they downplay any notion of superiority. One speaker will downplay her accomplishments, and the other is supposed to counteract it with praise and lift the person back up again. For example, one woman may say of an award she won, "I got lucky." The other woman will come back and say, "No, you worked hard, and you deserved it." However, women must become aware of and avoid downplaying words and phrases such as "I got lucky" or "It's no big deal."

The contributions of women are often overlooked in many organizations, which limits their advancement. However, in any arena in which you want to succeed, you must be visible. Being visible means speaking up during meetings and owning your accomplishments. On the other hand, being invisible means avoiding conflict, downplaying accomplishments, and failing to speak up when you should. The *Harvard Business Review* uses the term *intentional invisibility* to describe how women often choose to stay in the shadows to avoid any backlash they might face, particularly in a male-dominated environment.[2] They don't want to appear to be too independent or too pushy or rude; therefore, they moderate their behavior and dilute their strong personalities. While women understand that they need to stand out to get ahead, they also know that it exposes them to the risk of being labeled in a negative way. However, to truly be a leader, this tendency must be overcome.

In the book *Lean In*, Sheryl Sandberg and Marianne Cooper say that when a man is successful, he is well-liked, but when a woman is successful, she is liked less. Don't be deterred by such cultural norms. When it is your time to shine, shine brightly. Avoid downplaying language. Consider the "better way" responses in the following scenarios:

Scenario 1: Accepting Accolades

Susie: "Deborah, that was a really great message you just delivered on fear."

Deborah (playing small): "Oh, it wasn't me; it was God."

The Better Way: "Thank you so much. I am passionate about this subject because I was stuck in the prison of fear for so long. I now know the joy of being free, and I love telling others how they can be free too."

Scenario 2: When You Want to Put Forth a Solution to the Problem Being Discussed in a Group Meeting

Wrong Way (timidly speaking): "I may be wrong, but…"

The Better Way: "In light of the following facts, observations, and so on, I suggest that we consider doing (this). This will impact the situation this way…"

Strategies to Stop Playing Small

If you are used to playing small, now is the time to develop effective ways of overcoming this tendency. However, it can be daunting to change a behavior that has been ingrained in you. Try these strategies for getting on track:

1. *Stop using qualifiers.* Qualifiers are phrases such as "This is probably a bad idea, but…" or "I'm not sure this is right…" Using such qualifiers makes you sound tentative and less credible. If you sound like you doubt yourself, others may doubt you also. Of course, if your input is merely an unresearched suggestion, then don't be dogmatic about it. However, don't shoot down your own idea before you even present it. There are better ways to begin if you're not sure something will work, such as "My instinct is to do *XYZ*, but I need more time to think it through."

2. *Don't wait to be asked.* If you want to offer your services, participate in an event, or make a business presentation, don't wait for others to ask you. The only person who can make known what you want is you. Waiting to be asked can cause you to miss a great opportunity, so step up and make the first move. Recently, I served on a committee

to select a speaker for my college sorority's 50-year reunion. As we deliberated regarding who might deliver a 20-minute message within the allotted time, I confidently stated, "I've spoken in many time-sensitive venues. I can do it." They immediately approved. After the speech, one of my influential sorority sisters committed to using her influence to open other speaking doors for me.

3. *Say yes to new opportunities.* Stepping out of your comfort zone is never an easy thing. And if you're prone to downplaying your skills, you will be even more reluctant. The "Impostor Syndrome" (your inner critic that asks, "Who do you think you are to be doing such great things?") will goad you into thinking you can't possibly measure up. You must push yourself to embrace new opportunities to grow and improve. Even when you feel terrified at the prospect, you must start saying yes to opportunities that will stretch you. Don't allow fear to defeat you.

4. *Learn to accept no.* No one likes being told no, but those who play small let it derail their productivity and stifle their creativity. One person's no should not stop you from moving forward. Do not take it as a sign that you are incompetent or worthless; rejection is simply a part of life. As Albert Einstein is supposed to have said, "I am thankful for all of those who said No to me. It's because of them I'm doing it myself."

5. *Catch yourself in the act.* If you know you tend to self-deflect when being acknowledged for your accomplishments, you must start trying to catch yourself before you respond negatively. Take a moment to evaluate what you are going to say, and if it's anything other than gratitude, change the narrative in your head. If you have a Negative Nelly living inside your brain, now is the time to take steps to silence

her. A simple thank you is a great response when you feel the need to over talk.

Take a moment to evaluate what you are going to say, and if it's anything other than gratitude, change the narrative in your head.

---

6. *Don't allow criticism to cripple you.* You may receive a ton of positive feedback, but negative feedback can make you feel like it is the end of the world and not worth trying to move forward. You really can't please everyone, nor should you attempt to. Don't stop teaching just because some people might not like your message. Don't vow to stop writing because your book received a few bad reviews. If the criticism is constructive, make changes as appropriate, but don't quit.

7. *Get comfortable in the spotlight.* If you tend to minimize your skills, you often don't want to be the center of attention; after all, that is why you minimize them. For example, you may be at a networking event and someone asks you about yourself. Don't respond with a one-sentence answer and then turn the conversation back on them and their accomplishments. Take a few minutes to really expound on your message or product.

8. *Don't stifle your authentic self.* If you are a singer, don't try to imitate Whitney Houston. Find your voice and be uniquely you. You don't have to write like other authors or speak like other speakers. It is your uniqueness that will draw others to you, not your mimicking of those you feel are better than you. Remember, you are the only person who can excel at being you.

Owning Your Accomplishments

Many times, people downplay their accomplishments so they don't appear proud or conceited. While no one should literally pat themselves on the back, it is important to learn to graciously and confidently acknowledge your skills and speak up when you need to. Here are some strategies for embracing your accomplishments with class:

1. *Acknowledge your hard work.* If you've accomplished something major in your life, you likely did it with a lot of hard work. Therefore, do not downplay it or pretend that it was easy. Acknowledge the hard work you have done to get where you are.

2. *Don't put others down.* While you may want to acknowledge your accomplishments, never do so by putting anyone else down. Concentrate on what you have done rather than on what others have or have not done.

3. *Enjoy it.* You worked hard and it paid off. Or maybe the task wasn't hard but was something you're naturally good at. Whatever the case, enjoy the benefits that come with a major accomplishment. Give thanks to God who is the source of all gifts and abilities.

4. *Share the credit when necessary.* We often need the assistance of others to accomplish great things, so be sure to acknowledge those who helped you along the way whether it was a team of people, a partner, or even your family.

5. *Don't be overly confident.* While you don't want to downplay your accomplishments, you also don't want to appear conceited. No one likes the person who just knows they have it going on and they are better than anyone else. That means not saying things like, "I know." Acknowledge your accomplishments graciously.[3]

Sheryl Sandberg once worked for Google and, at the time of this writing, is now the chief operating officer of Facebook. She was told she was bossy her whole life and felt that she needed to hold back on being too successful or too smart. She says, "Women attribute their success to working hard, luck, and help from other people. Men will attribute that—whatever success they have, that same success, to their own core skills."[4]

Women have been socialized to dodge compliments; it's now time to forge a new model. Learn how to hear the accolades and mentally pass the credit to the true source of your excellence—the Almighty. As my friend popular author P. Bunny Wilson once said to me, "Praise is like perfume; if you consume it, it will kill you!"

FORSAKING WORK-LIFE BALANCE

*Beloved, I pray that you may prosper in all things
and be in health, just as your soul prospers.*

3 John 1:2 NKJV

I'm an *authorpreneur*, megachurch financial consultant, speaker, and leadership coach on demand. My schedule is as flexible as I determine it should be. And therein is the problem. There are no early morning corporate meetings to incentivize me to go to bed at a decent hour. Technological advances have made it possible for me to work anywhere at any time, but there have been times that I've gone overboard and worked everywhere all the time. I've always been one prone to operating with a full plate; I find it exhilarating. Thank God for my self-sufficient husband who is adamant about work-life balance and makes sure that I take time to smell the roses. But work is not all work for me; it is also play. Of course, I'm not the only one in my universe, so other people I care about require a lot of my time as well: ailing relatives, emotionally distressed friends, occasional houseguests, unending "pick your brain" requests from social media friends—you name it. Unfortunately, many of us women who are called to demanding professions or positions can easily find our lives out of balance. All too often, our "success" can be our failure, as it presents challenges to our health and domestic stability. We would be wise to make work-life balance our highest priority. Our most effective strategy for doing so is to maintain healthy boundaries, both personally and professionally.

How We Create or Allow Imbalance

Dr. Henry Cloud, coauthor of the popular book *Boundaries: When to Say Yes, How to Say No to Take Control of Your Life*, says, "A boundary is a personal property line, or limit, that defines where you end and someone else begins. Think of your home…There is a property line and you are in control of what goes on there, who is allowed to visit, and on and on. In short, you have control."[1] Without firmly expressed boundaries—with consequences—others will consistently trespass into our forbidden territory.

Without firmly expressed boundaries—
with consequences—others will consistently
trespass into our forbidden territory.

I have several friends, acquaintances, and associates who are pastors' wives. At a recent caucus with a group of them, there was a common thread of frustration over not having set proper boundaries with their congregations. Expectations were out of control. One woman lamented, "I still work a full-time job outside of the church, but the members expect me to attend every event we have!" They all agreed that trying to meet such expectations was overwhelming. Listen, ladies, it takes courage to set boundaries, especially on your time, but remember that it is *your* time. You have control over what you do or do not do. Don't let the fear of disapproval force you into the corner of resentment and exhaustion. Decide what you will be faithful to and be as consistent as you can. Remember that God loves a cheerful giver—not a tearful one. We are admonished in Psalm 100:2 (KJV) to "serve the LORD with gladness." What glory does God receive when we are serving people with a state of "madness" versus "gladness"? As a leader, we show others how to manage their lives by our example. Modeling balance is a great place to start.

Work-life strategist Tim Kehl explains,

> Achieving a healthy work-life balance requires managing our personal and professional life in sustainable ways that keep our energy flowing, our minds and bodies healthy, and our whole selves happy and content. It means giving due attention to all the things that enrich and fulfill us, including work and career, health and fitness, family and relationships, spirituality, community service, hobbies and passions, intellectual stimulation, and rest and recreation.[2]

Popular Chef Tommi Vincent is mastering the balancing act. She has settled in her heart that her priority is her family. Here is what she shared during our interview:

> The food industry is not family friendly. While others are celebrating holidays and momentous occasions, a chef is working. The thought of that gave me great pause. One of my nonnegotiables is I will not sacrifice my family for "success." For that reason, I created my own lane. My family's calendar goes in first. Then I work around my family.

Signs of Work-Life Imbalance

Often, when we are experiencing challenges in achieving a work-life balance, it shows. Here are some symptoms of imbalance:

1. *Exhaustion.* When we fail to establish proper boundaries in our work and personal lives, we experience both physical and mental exhaustion. Therefore, we become less productive and our ability to think clearly suffers.

2. *Missed activities.* Are you constantly missing your friends' birthday celebrations or your children's recitals or sports

games? Excessive absence at important events is a good indicator that your life is out of balance.

3. *No friends.* How are your friendships? Do you have any? If you find your circle of friends decreasing year after year because you are always too busy to hang out with them or talk on the phone, this is an indicator that your personal life is suffering due to a poor work-life balance. Nurture your friendships at all costs.

4. *Health problems.* If you have gained weight over a short period, experience frequent depression, have a substance addiction, are forgetful and unfocused, or are always tired, evaluate your work-life balance and get intentional about restoring order to your life.

Strategies for Achieving a Balanced Life

Many years ago, it was easy to draw a line between work and our personal lives. When we left the job at the end of the day, our work was done, and we were free to enjoy personal and family time. However, today, it is harder to leave our work behind when we are supposedly off the clock. Technology has made it easy for us to be on-call or simply to continue working once we get home. Unfortunately, we can be constantly connected to our jobs. We must realize that we have taught others how to treat us by what we allow. Fortunately, we still have the power of choice.

The most productive professionals are those with full and well-balanced lives. Consider these strategies for achieving a work-life balance:

1. *Identify areas of imbalance and poor time management.* From time to time, I set up a simple 24-hour log and enter how I'm spending my time. Recently, I was shocked to learn how much time I was investing in responding to social media and endless requests for brain-picking sessions from

numerous mentees and even people I'd never met. What I had sacrificed was adequate sleep, as it was often late into the evening before I got down to my "real work." No matter what your profession is, time is the great equalizer. Your success and ultimate fulfillment, personally and professionally, will be determined by how you manage yourself in this regard. Determine where your time is going.

2. *Reexamine your personal and professional priorities.* It's ironic that the things we often declare to be our top priorities often get relegated to the bottom of the list. For example, I always assert that prayer and exercise are my top priorities in a day. But there are times that my prayers become shorter and my exercise routine gets abandoned because of another more pressing "priority." Professionally, I have limited myself in my financial practice to a few, long-time clients. I consistently get calls to take on another. Doing so will certainly increase our bottom line but will just as surely affect one of my top priorities. Sometimes, we must choose to forego profits that could cause losses in other areas of our lives.

Sometimes, we must choose to forego profits that could cause losses in other areas of our lives.

---

3. *Seek accountability.* Once you have decided what your desired priorities are, solicit a friend, colleague, or even your spouse to help you stay on course. You may need a different person for each area of focus. I have a prayer partner to whom I've given permission to ask me, "How is your prayer life these days?" Another, asks, "How's your weight loss effort coming along?" Another keeps me

aware of my need to stay connected with my social media community and to respond to requests to submit articles. You will need to be proactive in seeking accountability partners because the average person will not volunteer for these not-so-easy tasks lest they offend you.

4. *Communicate your boundaries.* You can establish boundaries, but unless you communicate them, they will have no impact. Of course, the ideal time, professionally speaking, would be when you first join an organization or at the beginning of the relationship. However, that's hindsight. One of my boundaries is that Friday afternoons/evenings are reserved for my weekly date night. I don't work late on this day, nor do I schedule time with my friends. Everyone is aware of this. Some "forget" and call me on Fridays. Since I'm determined not to teach people that it's okay to violate my established boundaries, I usually do not answer the phone. Or, I may respond with a quick text, "Do you have an emergency? This is date night."

5. *Maintain a 360-degree mind-set regarding work-life balance.* Imagine your life as a stool with a base and four legs. The base will be the principles, values, and core beliefs that guide your actions. The legs represent the physical, relational, emotional, and financial pillars of your life. You cannot afford to make a single "leg" your top priority. Each leg is critical to a balanced, fulfilled, and productive existence. So don't let your quest to achieve perfection in one area sabotage another. For example, physical health is critical, but don't choose working out over praying. Don't tolerate toxic relationships and end up depressed about being a doormat. Don't attempt to save every dollar you make and never enjoy a good vacation or a nice dinner out with family and friends. If you neglect a single one of the legs on your life stool, you will experience an imbalance that will thwart a fulling life.

During my interview with Dr. Aimee Sanchez, neuropsychologist and leadership coach, she offered this practical insight into her work-life balancing routine:

> Priorities for me are something that I have to be introspective about. I have to take an internal assessment from minute to minute. If I'm feeling anxious, I have to do something in my body to recognize that and then self-correct. When I was younger, I used to think going to bed at 8:30 p.m. was early. To me, that's late now. Occasionally, I'll stay up too late, but I noticed on the next day that it affects me. So I try to go to bed early consistently. I make sure that my house is quiet, that everything is settled down by that time. That enables me the following day to be able to get up and have the presence of mind to do what I need to do.

Achieving a healthy work-life balance doesn't necessarily mean making a lot of big changes at once. This will only overwhelm you. Instead, begin to make small changes in a way that improves the quality of your life. Remember that work-life balance will look different for everyone. What's right for someone else isn't necessarily right for you. Evaluate your own life and figure out what you need and want (for example, a housekeeping service or virtual assistant), and then arrange your priorities (financial and other) to serve those needs. You must stand strong as the guardian of your purposes, goals, values, and life.

LACKING EXECUTIVE PRESENCE

*How we look, what we present, and how we
present it are the essence of executive presence.*

—Deborah Smith Pegues

"Strong executive presence" was the first thought that came to mind
when I met Shirley Hoogstra at a meeting of a national religious nonprofit organization in Washington, DC, where she had been invited
to make a presentation. She clearly knew her stuff and was passionate
about the work she was doing as president of the Council for Christian Colleges and Universities. In addition to her obvious intellect
and enthusiasm, I was struck by her relatability. Even though she was
a seasoned attorney and a former partner in an East Coast law firm,
Shirley did not speak in legalese. She presented her information in a
clear, direct manner that made the issues immediately comprehen-
sible. Later, when I complimented her on her attractive boots, she
shared information on how I could order a pair. Talk about being personable! Even as she networked with other attendees later, her mag-
netic personality commanded the room. Curious to know her secrets
for developing such executive presence, I quickly scheduled an interview with her when I started writing this book. Our conversation was
rewarding and empowering. Here is a snippet.

Me: Shirley, what aspect of your upbringing helped you
develop the executive presence you so clearly exhibit?

Shirley: My mother was a real leader even though she was a woman of the '50s and '60s, where that was very hard to effectuate outside the home. My dad ran his own business. If you were a successful family, your wife stayed home. Plus she had five children. There was very little time, but she had such natural authority. She was the president of the women's circle at church. She was on a library board. So I saw both of my parents being real leaders in the spheres in which they operated. Although I grew up in the '60s and '70s, I was not raised in a chauvinist home. My father, the eighth and youngest son of an immigrant family, had three sisters who were all in business. So that was even more important because in the '30s, '40s, and '50s, here were his sisters who worked in the family business. I grew up with a freedom that was not stifled by expectations or stereotypes.

Shirley's upbringing had positioned her to be comfortable around people of authority and power. Thus she exuded executive presence with ease.

Asked to define what executive presence is, many executives, recruiters, or other evaluators stumble when trying to articulate a concrete description. In denying promotions, they usually resort to such statements as "She just isn't management material" or "She doesn't come across strong enough." I've certainly been privy to such conversations about high-potential employees who lacked executive presence.

Sometimes, executive presence is better explained by its absence. Such was the case with "Lorna." She was a smart cookie. She headed the internal audit department of a famous Fortune 500 company. She had previously worked for one of the then "Big Eight" (now Big Four) certified public accounting (CPA) firms and had almost achieved partner status. Lorna seemed to care little about her appearance. Frumpy clothes, no makeup, and stained teeth from smoking were her norm. Not only was she a visual mess, but she was also unlikable. She was arrogant, curt, and impatient with people whom she did not deem to be as smart as she was. She labeled almost everyone she interacted with an "idiot." At her next job, her staff frequently commented about her obviously poor self-image behind her back. Lorna never got promoted to chief financial officer—the next-level position for which she was well qualified. Company employees generally assumed it was because she lacked executive presence.

Women who want to maximize their potential as leaders cannot dismiss this important element. There are numerous books, executive coaches, finishing schools, YouTube videos, and other resources available that can help you develop in this area. A quick internet search is a good place to start. Based on my four decades of experience as a vice president and CFO and having held other executive roles in various profit and nonprofit entities, here are the five areas that I recommend you focus on for a self-assessment of where you are in your development of executive presence.

Proficiency

Are you known for being knowledgeable and excellent in your field of expertise? People with executive presence not only excel within the scope of their job function, but they are also diligent in expanding their perspective and gaining an understanding of the political, technological, cultural, or other factors that impact their entities and their role in particular. They are proactive in recommending or implementing measures to mitigate the impact of these forces on their effectiveness and profitability. They invest time and money in their personal development by subscribing to publications or podcasts and participating in outside organizations that keep them up to date on the cutting edge of trends for their industry. What efforts are you putting forth in this area? Do you know what the forecast for your industry or area of interest is for the next five years?

Powerfulness

Do you project the image of having the capability or power to handle special situations with cool confidence? This aspect of executive presence goes beyond being confident of your ability to fulfill the duties of your job description. It is your readiness to handle a crisis or adverse situation. Let's start with something minor like restoring order after you've allowed a few minutes of interaction among the participants during your presentation. I'm amazed at the number of women I see who are uncomfortable simply asking the audience to stop talking—and refusing to proceed until they do so. Why, I've asked people engaged in sidebar conversations to wrap it up if they are distracting the other participants. Sometimes, I'll take a light-hearted approach and say, "Hey, I work alone so I need all eyes up here." I've been known to ask, "Is there a question I can answer? I want us all to stay on the same page." Besides, I usually warn folks at the beginning of a presentation that I prefer all comments to be held and directed to me when I offer the Q&A session.

I've been in small group meetings where the leader has allowed one aggressive participant to change the agenda for the day. I've seen meeting hosts too timid to alert a speaker that she has exceeded her time limit. And how would you respond if all the electrical power went out in the middle of the keynote speaker's message? These are all scenarios that I have witnessed. You display executive presence when you can "think on your feet" and calmly propose a solution to whatever arises. Listen, ladies, when you are in charge, act like it. You'll never get the respect you deserve if you don't exercise your authority. This doesn't mean being demanding or reminding everyone that you are in charge. Your confidence and demeanor should command rather than demand respect. If you do not lead, there are others who will assume authority because they cannot stand to watch a leader default on her responsibility. Remember that leaders lead.

You display executive presence when you can "think on your feet" and calmly propose a solution to whatever problem arises.

Packaging

How have you chosen to package yourself? Does your wardrobe align with your industry's standard and the values you proclaim? How do the women on the fast track in your organization or profession dress?

In addition to corporate engagements, I speak in various churches cross-culturally and cross-denominationally. Some are very conservative and specifically forbid women speakers to wear pants. Others are very liberal—and adamant about speakers projecting a "youthful" image to be relatable to their younger generation. I choose to be sensitive to and accommodate their requirements to the extent they do not violate my own standards of how I present myself. I don't have the luxury of ignoring their guidelines in the name of "just being me."

The goal of wise personal packaging is to not be distracting to your message. Every woman does not package herself like "Lorna," whom you met earlier in this chapter. Some go to the other extreme. You may not agree with what I'm about to say but hear me out—especially if you work in a male-dominated environment. *Cleavage, short or tight-fitting attire, and other "figure-emphasizing" outfits will sabotage your message and your image.* This is a huge problem that some women would rather not discuss. In her book *The Male Factor: The Unwritten Rules, Misperceptions, and Secret Beliefs of Men in the Workplace,* social researcher Shaunti Feldhahn reports the results of testing thousands of men to determine if their focus was impacted by a female presenter's choice of attire. In the testing, when the woman dressed attractively rather than provocatively, the men had a higher rate of retention of her information.[1] Feldhahn goes on to explain that men are wired to notice a seductive female—even when it's not her primary intention to be so.

It is very common in Hollywood for women to wear revealing outfits. I noticed a difference, however, in how filmmaker / director / leadership speaker Ava DuVernay dresses. I asked her about it during our interview:

Me: Ava, you are a beautiful woman and I noticed in reviewing countless online photos of you attending various events that you appear to have found that sweet spot for dressing attractively but not provocatively. Is that intentional? Are you being careful not to sabotage your power by dressing in a way that calls attention to your physicality?

Ava: I think women can dress however they want. For me though, because I am a director and I'm in a leadership position, I dress more conservatively to help people focus on what I'm saying as opposed to other things. I don't think that there's anything wrong with anyone dressing the way they want. I think people should feel comfortable. I just feel comfortable being a little bit more covered up.

Yes, ladies, you could assert that men shouldn't be looking at women in that manner and that this is just one more instance in which women have to accommodate them in order to succeed, but I would caution all women to pursue the path that advances your ball down the court. Choose between being taken seriously versus being perceived as a visual thrill. Know that people (men and women) will remember you by what you make memorable. To develop executive presence, make sure your message is more memorable than your outfit. See chapter 24 for additional discussion on this topic.

People Skills

Being personable, relatable, and likable are essential to achieving executive presence. Let's face it. In the final analysis, all goals and objectives must be achieved through people. Therefore, whatever your profession, solid people skills will be one of the most empowering tools in your arsenal. It's no secret that everyone prefers to do business and socialize with people they like. In my book *The One-Minute Money Mentor for Women,*[2] I discuss various ways you can become more likable. As you review the abbreviated list below, consider which skills you need to hone and which ones you can be grateful that the grace of God is prevailing in that area of your life.

- *Smile.* A smile will brighten your day as well as that of those you encounter. Smiling is a universal language that never requires an interpreter. Of course, it's no effort to smile when things are going well, but make every effort to look pleasant even when things are not going so great.

- *Remember common courtesies.* Say "thank you" and "please" to everyone. Request rather than command or demand what you desire from others.

- *Listen.* Be intentionally silent for periods of time during a conversation and make eye contact, nod, and listen. Show genuine interest in other people. Ask clarifying questions as appropriate. Be conscious of the number of times you say "I" during your conversations. Don't allow the conversation to be all about you.

- *Respect other people's right to believe and behave differently.* No need to be adamant about noneternal matters or those that do not affect the quality of your life. Keep your disdain and critical judgments to yourself. Steer clear of political and religious discussions. You never know where others really stand so just listen graciously if a higher-up or client insists on engaging in such a conversation. Have some safe, stock responses ready: "I'm just grateful to live in such a great country" or "I am praying for everyone in authority."

- *Do not interrupt.* Even if a person is long-winded. If you feel you need to interject a point, raise your index finger slightly as if to ask for permission to speak. If that doesn't work, try to jump into the conversation at the end of their thought.

- *Be humble.* Humility is not an affected demeanor; it is a mind-set, an inner acknowledgment of the true source of all your skills and abilities. It tops the chart as the most admired character trait; pride and arrogance are the most detestable. So don't brag about your position, possessions, people you know, or places you've traveled.

- *Admit your mistakes.* Trying to place blame on others will earn you the label of "first-class jerk." Be confident and humble enough to say, "I was wrong." It will increase rather than decrease your personal stock in the eyes of others.

- *Make every effort to remember people's names.* A person's name can be the sweetest and most important sound in any language. It makes them feel significant when you remember them.

- *Always make the other person feel valued and appreciated.* Do it sincerely and without hidden motives. Phoniness is more discernable than you think. Simply acknowledge or praise employees' small and large acts of service and their accomplishments.

We can always study more, obtain one more degree or certification, and make other attempts to increase our competency. While practical knowledge may get you in the door, good people skills are essential in moving you forward. Your care and concern for others can result in your becoming a charismatic leader with strong executive presence.

Presentation Prowess

Does your communication style command attention when you take the stage or make a presentation? If you do not possess good presentation skills, you are going to be hard-pressed to get anyone to embrace your ideas, plans, or proposals. This area is so critical to executive presence that I'm going to devote the entire next chapter to our tendency as women to "weak-speak."

SPEAKING LIKE A WEAKLING

*Speech is power, speech is to persuade,
to convert, to compel.*

—Ralph Waldo Emerson, American philosopher and poet

As you advance in your profession and gain increasing influence, you will be called on to speak in public, to present ideas and proposals to clients, to motivate followers, or to inform or inspire others. "Presentation prowess" is a critical component of executive presence. Like any other undertaking, you learn and get good at it with practice. Therefore, you'll want to run toward every opportunity to develop your speaking and presentation skills. Toastmasters International (toastmasters.org) is a safe place to start—in the company of others with the common goal of mastering public speaking. If you do not have access to a local chapter, try watching YouTube videos or other recordings of great speakers. I have found public speaking to be one of the most rewarding endeavors I've ever undertaken. I've not attained perfection in this area by any means, but I humbly enjoy the frequent standing ovations.

Tips for Speaking with Power

Below is a summary of the most significant tips and strategies that have served me well and some behaviors that have not in my quest to strengthen my executive presence.

Present with Conviction

To project strong executive presence and to command the room, you must believe and be fully sold on your message. Be clear on what you are "selling" and what makes you unique in selling it. For public speaking, practice, practice, practice—using bullet points only. Resist the temptation to memorize your message verbatim. The goal is for you to sound authentic and relatable and not rehearsed. So practice presenting thoughts instead of words. An audience can sense your discomfort and may not embrace your message if you do not appear to buy into it yourself. Know that they want you to succeed and are rooting for you. Most of all, remember that you have the omnipresent God empowering you to win.

To project strong executive presence and
to command the room, you must believe
and be fully sold on your message.

Eliminate "Up Talk"

Does your voice go up at the end of your statements making it sound as if you are asking a question rather than making a declaration? Drop this habit now; it makes you sound tentative and uncertain of what you are saying. Overcome this tendency by taping your talks or soliciting the help of a friend or colleague. Consciously drop your voice at the end of a sentence to give it certainty. Even when introducing yourself, say your name slowly and clearly with an air of finality. "Hello, I'm Deborah Smith Pegues." Lower your pitch slightly on your last name. Proceed to offer other information about yourself but try not to include it in the same sentence as your name. This gives the hearer the opportunity to allow your name to sink in.

Speak Louder

If your volume is too low, it will negate all your research and planning, since no one will hear you. Voice projection is critical. You will not be judged as being "too masculine" by speaking loudly enough to be heard—in a pleasant, non-yelling tone, of course. The key here is in proper breathing from your diaphragm (the muscle that rests below your lungs). You can practice by pretending your abdomen is a balloon that fills up with air when you inhale slowly. Your shoulders and chest should not rise. When you exhale, your abdomen should deflate. There are numerous YouTube illustrations of how this works, so a quick search for "diaphragmatic breathing" will get you on the path.

Of course, I'm a big advocate of investing in professional training, so I recommend at least a couple of recorded sessions with a voice coach who can evaluate your speech deficiencies and instruct you on how to eliminate them. In the meantime, stand in a room and pretend to "shoot your voice" to a designated spot using the force of the air in your diaphragm. You may simply say your name or make a statement. Get used to hearing yourself sound stronger. If you tend to speak in a high-pitched voice, you may want to consider lowering your tone a bit to sound more authoritative. The goal is not to sound like a man but rather a woman who wants to be heard.

Speak Slowly

Speaking too fast has been my biggest challenge—a trait my siblings and I inherited from our father. In my effort to always adhere to my allotted speaking time, I have frequently increased my pace. I try to mitigate the impact by clearly articulating my words; however, I'm sure that on those occasions when I "speed speak" I reach the finish line long before the audience—if they ever do. I've improved significantly as I've learned how important it is to allow the audience to absorb what I'm saying. Pausing is a powerful strategy. I'm really motivated to continue to grow in this area as I watch "a-ha moments" register on people's faces versus the frantic expression that says, "I didn't catch all you just said!" A deliberate pace and an intentional pause are especially critical when speaking to a culturally diverse audience, some of whom must interpret *and* comprehend the application of your message.

Get to the Point

Maybe I am a bottom-line person because I have worked in male-dominated environments most of my professional life. I find it really challenging to listen to the long version of a story. Several of my male friends have often complained that most women just can't seem to tell the essence of a story. I agree with them. If this describes you, try these strategies.

- *Start with the End in Mind*
  Ask yourself, "What is the main thought I want to convey?" Rather than building up to it, consider stating it upfront and then supporting it with brief facts and observations.

- *Recognize and avoid "rabbit trails."*
  Do not veer off the path of your main point by introducing a point or idea that does not add clarity to the message or discussion at hand. Stories (especially personal ones) and anecdotes are priceless, but they must always, always be relevant and must reinforce your point.

- *Don't Overwhelm the Audience*
  Presenting too many points, too many PowerPoint slides, or other information is a killer to your effectiveness. It's best to select and develop one to three points if you want your talk to be remembered. I attended a presentation once where the speaker highlighted, during his 30-minute talk, 20 ways to be successful. I was overwhelmed from the moment he announced his plan to cover so much information.

Responding When a Man Hijacks Your Idea

It happens with such frequency that we don't need to spend time bemoaning the unfairness of it. You put forth an idea, and it gets a lukewarm reception. Within minutes, a man repeats it and gets praised for it. Want to put an end to it? Here's my suggested script for responding when a man "he-peats" your input: Turn to him and calmly, pleasantly, but boldly say, "Thank you, John, for reiterating that. I appreciate it." "Now (turning back toward the group), just to reemphasize…" Proceed to further amplify your original statement. You can choose to make a restatement with little or no modification. Being a broken record is okay if you keep the tone positive. Remember that you cross the stereotype line if you show extreme anger, leaving the men wondering, "What's up with her?" During our interview, Barry Knight—CEO of BEK Impact Company, a popular leadership coaching firm, and author of *Impactability*—confirmed my theory.

Me: Barry, you've heard the continuing complaint that men often hijack women's ideas and get the credit for them during meetings. What would you think if you observed such an incident and the woman immediately exclaimed to the perpetrator, "I just said that!"

Barry: I would think to myself, "What's with the attitude? Why is she getting so emotional?" Once a woman comes on that strong, we tend to diminish her because she is not operating like a lady. I think we forget that if the lady is a leader, she has just as much right to put forth her idea and to self-advocate if she needs to take back ownership.

What if your original idea or statement was not made during the current meeting but you had shared your input with John in a prior discussion or brainstorming session? He now brings it to the table as his original idea. How do you gracefully take back ownership? Try this script:

"John, thanks for reiterating our prior discussion. Since I shared that initial idea with you, I have also learned that…" This is the time to put forth a related fact, stat, study, or other reference to show that you have thoroughly considered, studied, and investigated the issue. Always have a relevant fact ready to add to the discussion or even a plan B. Again, say it boldly—but always calmly. Women, especially in high powered positions, don't always get the luxury of showing anger or any other negative emotion without being judged negatively for doing so. It's our reality for now so just learn to manage it. Move on.

Eliminating Credibility Robbers

There are certain words and phrases that sabotage your presentation and your credibility as a powerful professional. Here are the ones I've observed most often:

- *"Okay?" or "right?"* I was part of a women's empowerment group where the coach always annoyingly ended her statements with "Right?" I wanted to yell, "Are you asking us to validate what you are teaching us? Are you the authority or not!" Of course, I resisted the temptation. I did, however, lovingly call it to her attention—privately, of course, but she continued the habit. I tried to grin and bear it; I couldn't wait for the training to end.

- *Fillers ("ah," "'em," "uh," "really," "actually," "basically").* These words have no substance and are annoying to the discriminating listener. To conquer this habit, try pausing and collecting your thoughts rather than filling the space with a filler while you wait for the thought to arrive. A brief silence can be golden. Just look pensive and don't stare at the ceiling.

- *Excessive repetition.* When you use words and phrases such as "awesome," "wow," "no kidding," "get out of here," and so forth repeatedly, you sound unprofessional and in need of vocabulary expansion. Even when praying in public, many women—and men—have a habit of excessively repeating God's name at the end of each phrase or sentence. Example: "We thank you this morning, Father God, for your many blessings, Father God. And Father God, we ask you to be with us today, Father God, as we go out into the world, Father God…" Such praying style can be tedious and annoying to listen to. Remember that prayer is simply talking to God. You can speak to him using an everyday conversational style. Of course, you can talk to him in any way you please, but in public settings, where many people may not be accustomed to such repetitiveness, you will want to avoid it. To understand the full impact of this recommendation, try rereading the foregoing example and substituting "John" or your best friend's name instead of "Father God." Would you really call their name that many times?

- *Unnecessary apologies.* Are you one of those women who constantly apologizes—even for things beyond your control? Shed this habit by asking yourself the following questions before you say, "I'm sorry":

    ○ "Did I cause the negative circumstance that I'm about to apologize for?"

    ○ "Am I really sorry (remorseful), or am I trying to be empathetic?"

    ○ "What can I say instead of 'I'm sorry' to convey my concern?"

My suggestion for breaking the "sorry" habit is to replace it with an alternative. Acknowledge that a situation is unfortunate without taking responsibility for it. For example, instead of saying, "I'm sorry that the snowstorm caused us to cancel the training seminar," try saying, "Unfortunately, Mother Nature had different plans." Of course, an apology is indeed in order when you have caused someone to be disadvantaged or inconvenienced in any way.

- *Speaking "out-of-school."* Stick to what you know for sure when you offer input. When I asked Phil Cooke, film-maker, cofounder of Cooke Media Group, and media consultant to secular organizations and megaministries, to weigh in on ways he has observed women sabotage themselves in the workplace, he explained,

  > I love working with women. I've hired more women in my career than men. I've also fired a few women. One of the most common reasons has been for over-communicating—talking in meetings when they had no clue what they were talking about. I had an employee who wanted desperately to contribute to the conversation during our client meetings. So from day one, she would go into a meeting knowing noth-ing about our past projects or the progress we'd made. Therefore, when she would interject (and she couldn't help herself), she would make inappropriate state-ments that made us all look like idiots. I talked to her multiple times and asked her to keep quiet until she was on the job longer and knew more, but she simply couldn't shut up. I've never seen anything like it. So I finally had to let her go.
  >
  > As women move into more positions of influence, they can become so eager to look like they deserve a place at the table, they may try too hard. Sometimes it's better to keep quiet for the short term, learn all you can, and then assert yourself.

- *Profanity.* The words you choose affect how you are per-ceived. In some workplaces, profanity is the norm. You must be careful to guard against allowing your environment to set the standard for your language. Some women use four-letter expletives and justify doing so by saying the words are in the Bible (e.g., "damn," "hell"). Think about the potential damage to your reputation and to your personal witness before releasing those macho, tough-guy-sounding words. In my book *30 Days to Taming Your Tongue*, I devote an entire chapter to challenging readers to abstain from cussing. If you think such admonitions are unnecessary in a book targeting women, think again!

As you practice and embrace the foregoing suggestions, you will begin to eliminate these credibility robbing traps and tendencies. You will project authority, confidence, and competence to people you meet for the first time as well as to superiors, colleagues, customers, constituents, and employees.

FAILING TO ENGAGE CONSTRUCTIVE FEEDBACK

*If you listen to constructive criticism, you
will be at home among the wise.*

Proverbs 15:31

"Susan," a 68-year-old independent marketing coach, was fuming after her discussion with 25-year-old "Nicole," whom she had hired to manage her social media platforms. When Susan pushed back regarding a grammatically incorrect post that Nicole had issued on her behalf, Nicole insisted that it was perfectly okay in today's culture for wording, punctuation, and so on to be imperfect. She further stated that Susan had a "generational knowledge gap" about the issue. Being a highly regarded and seasoned professional, Susan was put off by Nicole's insensitive and judgmental words—especially considering her limited experience. Good grammar was in Susan's DNA. English instructors from grade school through grad school had drilled into her the importance of using proper grammar and how the failure to do so would likely influence people's perception of her intelligence. After a few deep breaths, Susan wisely decided to let go of her anger and to insist on approving all posts before they were released to the public.

Giving and receiving feedback can be uncomfortable for both parties, since you don't have any guarantee as to how the other person will respond. Notwithstanding, a leader cannot default on this daunting task as it is critical to achieving personal and professional objectives. In my books *Confronting Without Offending* and *30 Days to a Stronger, More Confident You*, I explain strategies for moving beyond the fear of being alienated or not being liked to regularly addressing issues that thwart unity and effectiveness. Let's examine a few.

Keys to Giving Constructive Feedback

What a wonderful world it would be if every person had 20/20 vision with respect to their inefficiencies and failings—and knew exactly how to correct them. A good leader, though personally flawed, will understand that constructive feedback is one of the best gifts she can extend to those under her authority or in her circle of influence. Here are some winning guidelines to follow:

What a wonderful world it would be if every person had 20/20 vision with respect to their inefficiencies and failings—and knew exactly how to correct them.

- *Give the feedback promptly.* If you delay, your silence could be interpreted as approval of the undesired behavior. You will surely get resistance after people have established a pattern, since we teach people how to behave by what we tolerate.

- *Give the feedback personally.* Go directly to the person yourself—always face-to-face when possible. No one will appreciate knowing you have shared his shortcomings with everybody else before you told him. Tell him what you have observed personally. Don't hide behind what "they" are saying.

- *Give the feedback privately.* Be sure that no one else is around to hear your conversation. Giving feedback in the presence of others will only cause the person to be so concerned with saving face that she may not absorb a word you say. Find a quiet place where you can discuss the issues without interruption.

- *Maintain a "constructive" purpose.* At all times, the leader's goal must be to build or develop the recipient and not to tear down or be critical.

- *Use encouraging words.* Doing so shows that you support and believe in the recipient's ability to change.

- *Clarify exactly what is expected or the standard that is not being met.* Give specific actionable suggestions as to what the person can do. This is critical especially when you give feedback to a woman.

Women often receive less—and less helpful—feedback. While men get specific recommendations for improving their performance, women hear more generic feedback that's harder to act on, such as "Good job" or "You need more presence in meetings." Men may hesitate to give critical feedback to women for fear of eliciting an emotional response—and this is likely the case for women too. Unfortunately, this lack of input hinders a woman's progress. It's hard to build skills and advance if you are not aware of your specific shortcomings. Look for opportunities to give the women you work with input that can help them learn and grow. Remember that holding back for fear you'll upset someone doesn't benefit her.[1]

You are already aware of exactly what they need to do; therefore, communicate it "sandwich style": Bread (affirmation) + meat *(problem / recommended solution)* + bread (more affirmation).

Here is an example:

Bread: "Jackie, I appreciate your creativity in setting up the book table and the friendly way you greet the customers."

Meat: "I notice that the buyers tend to engage you in extended conversations that hold up the line. We will sell a lot more product if you could minimize the small talk and gently urge them along."

Bread: "Your being so relatable is a real asset to our operation."

- *Anticipate defensiveness:* The average person harbors some level of insecurity or inadequacy about an aspect of their being, so they often feel any kind of feedback confirms their inferiority. Therefore, it is highly unlikely that they will respond by saying, "You are absolutely right in your assessment of my shortcomings. Thank you so much for pointing it out." That's why it's important to cite specific times and instances of the behavior you find problematic. Don't be put off by the defensiveness. It's human nature to resist the pain of the truth.

Receiving Constructive Criticism

Just like the people who get defensive when you confront them regarding their deficiencies, you also lack 20/20 vision on your shortcomings. And while the same guidelines apply when the table is turned, you have no control over how someone chooses to deliver their "criticism" of you. Therefore, you must decide in advance to always frame the feedback as a positive experience—even though the truth hurts.

I once worked as vice president of a venture capital firm and assisted the president in negotiating the terms of our investments in various start-up companies. During our meetings with the entrepreneurs, I would propose the financing terms but had the hardest time being comfortable with the silence that followed. Thus I would jump back in and offer a slight compromise before the entrepreneur could respond to the initial offer. Although my boss appreciated my ability to analyze the deals, put forth creative terms, and present them, he explained that I was shooting us in the foot by not letting the silence hang out there. Being a talkative person in my personal life, this was clearly a female trait that I had to get under control. It took some time, but I finally learned to present the offer and zip my lips—especially after I realized the pregnant, awkward silence was one of the entrepreneur's negotiating tactics. I am forever grateful to my boss for his courage in confronting me, the caring manner in which he did, and his specific recommendation to take a negotiating class.

In receiving feedback, you will demonstrate emotional and spiritual maturity when you do the following:

- *Listen.* Relax your defenses. Don't interrupt. Ask the confronter to cite specific instances and examples of the problem. Let your body language communicate that you are seeking to understand and to grow as a result of the conversation. Keep a pleasant expression. Do not cross your arms (in defiance), smirk, sigh, or roll your eyes.

- *Look.* See if there is a kernel of truth in what is being said. Don't dismiss it or take it as a personal attack. Know that when a person (even a non-boss) has the courage to point out your weakness, it is usually for your good. The truth will set you free.

- *Learn.* There is a developmental lesson in receiving constructive feedback, so welcome people who challenge your thinking. Be eager to gain a broader perspective.

- *Leave.* Some criticism is not constructive but groundless and downright destructive. When you have listened closely and looked for the kernel of truth, but found none, simply say, "Thank you for your input; I'll take it from here." You handle this kind of feedback much the way you eat bony fish; you eat the flesh and leave the bones. Don't spend time rehearsing the encounter, trying to decipher motives. Stay focused on your objectives.

Speaking Truth to Power

Many leaders, especially those in the religious community, are often put off by followers or subordinates who express their concern or disagreement with their actions. They are quick to accuse dissenters of "not supporting the ministry." The truth is that every leader needs a "Jethro." As Moses's father-in-law, Jethro, grew concerned when he saw Moses burning himself out handling every minor and major problem the Israelites brought to him during their journey to the Promised Land. He wasted no time in telling him, "What you are doing is not good."[2] Moses was so enmeshed in the details that he had not realized the gravity of the problem. Jethro went on to recommend a specific solution to the dilemma that involved a system of delegating the bulk of the problem-solving to others. The moral of the story is that every leader would be wise to surround herself with people who have the courage to speak truth to those in power.

When you lead like a woman, you treat feedback as a gift whether you are the giver or the receiver. Give and seek it often and watch your career soar.

EXPECTING INSTEAD OF ASKING

To be passive is to let others decide for you. To be aggressive is to decide for others. To be assertive is to decide for yourself. And to trust that you are enough.

Dr. Edith Eva Eger, Holocaust survivor and author of *The Choice*

How many times have you heard a woman say of her husband or significant other, "He *should* know what I want without me having to tell him"? While those in romantic relationships tend to get familiar with each other's desires over time, it is unrealistic to expect another person to know exactly what we want—in personal and professional relationships. Women in leadership will often assume their superiors and even their subordinates will know what they expect. It's magical thinking to believe that a boss will recognize that you deserve and desire certain benefits, recognition, or rewards and will grant them without prompting.

Women are reluctant to speak up in general; many feel they do it at their peril. Sheryl Sandberg and Adam Grant, authors of *Option B,* said in a *New York Times* article, "We've both seen it happen again and again. When a woman speaks in a professional setting, she walks a tightrope. Either she is barely heard, or she is judged as too aggressive. When a man says virtually the same thing, heads nod in appreciation for his fine idea. As a result, women often decide that saying less is more."[1] Women worry about the social consequences of asking for something. If they think the costs of asking outweigh the benefits, they tend to keep silent.

Women are more likely to hesitate before they ask for something if others might perceive them as being greedy or too demanding. The KPMG Women's Leadership Study reveals that failure to ask for what we want stems from a lack of confidence. "One in four working women (25 percent) report that not asking for what they want held them back from advancing in their career."

> Women are more likely to hesitate before they ask for something if others might perceive them as being greedy or too demanding.

Consider the following statistics:

- 92 percent don't feel comfortable asking for sponsorship.
- 79 percent lack confidence in seeking mentors.
- 76 percent fail to ask for access to senior leadership.
- 73 percent don't pursue job opportunities beyond their level of experience.
- 65 percent won't ask for a promotion.
- 61 percent don't ask for a raise they feel they deserve.
- 56 percent fail to ask for a new role or position.[2]

In the book *Women Don't Ask* by Linda Babcock and Sara Laschever, Linda, who is an economics professor at Carnegie Mellon University, tells the story of when she was director of the university's PhD program. A group of female students complained that all the male PhD candidates were teachers, while all the women were only teaching assistants. They didn't think it was fair and neither did Linda. When Linda asked the associate dean about this, he said the men had asked for teaching positions and the women had not. The men knew what they wanted and boldly went to the associate dean with their request. On the other hand, the women were expecting an email asking if they wanted to teach.[3] Linda says that women have been conditioned from an early age to "wait for things to be offered to them," and this spills over into professional environments. Little girls are taught that it's not appropriate to focus on their wants and pursue things for their own self-interest.[4]

My Story: You Have Not Because You Ask Not

I was hired as chief financial officer by an organization that had embarked on a huge building project, but the financing had not been secured. My job was to negotiate the best possible financing package—which I did. The company also hired a construction manager to oversee the project. I worked many long hours including holidays to bring the transaction to fruition. The construction manager worked regular hours and hired independent contractors from time to time to facilitate his responsibilities—which was a smart move for work-life balance. I, on the other hand, consistently worked 10- to 12-hour days, refusing to replace needed personnel in my department. I made every effort to increase our bottom line and pave the way for the required cash flow to qualify for the upcoming financing. At the year-end board of director's meeting, the board asked the construction manager to step out of the room while they discussed how much to give him as a bonus; they voted to give him a substantial amount. No one said a word about rewarding all my efforts and budget-cutting accomplishments with a bonus. I was livid. Like the Proverbs 31 woman, I did indeed "perceive that my merchandise was good." I knew that the skills I brought to the table were invaluable to the organization and could not be easily found in the marketplace. I knew I was trustworthy and committed to the organization's leadership and its goals. So I spoke up. "I'm going to step out now and give you an opportunity to discuss my bonus," I said with a pleasant but matter-of-fact tone. Talk about an awkward moment. The silence was so thick, you could have cut it with a knife. Results? They voted to give me a comparable bonus. Mission accomplished. I'm a firm believer that you have not because you ask not.

Tips for Asking for What You Want

It's time to ask for what you want. Since no isn't fatal, what's the worst that could happen? Try these strategies for a positive outcome:

Do your research. The more difficult your request, the more you need to be prepared. The answer to almost every question you have can be found through a simple Google search. If you want a higher salary, research the pay for your position in your industry and be prepared to explain why you deserve (versus *need*) a raise. Keep a file of all your accomplishments, extra projects, cost savings recommended, and so on throughout the year to present as support for your request. Practice what and how you will ask so you can confidently present your request. This is not the time to be modest; you are not *bragging* on yourself, you are *reporting* the results of your efforts.

Be specific. One of the biggest stumbling blocks to getting a yes is that we are often vague about what we want. "I need a raise." Would a 1 percent increase be okay? After all, it is a raise. Don't be vague in giving your subordinate an assignment; be clear as to your expected outcome so that you get what you want when you want it.

Be reasonable. We should ask for what we want, but this doesn't mean we can be unreasonable. This is where your research will serve you best. Know the norms and trends for your industry and environment. If you have access to the organization's annual or quarterly financial report, review it. Ask a knowledgeable outsider to help you interpret it if you are not skilled at doing so. The organization may not be in the financial position to grant raises for now.

Believe you are worth it. Often, we don't make requests because deep down we don't believe we are worth it. I'm endeavoring to always be of the mind-set of the woman in Proverbs 31: *She perceives that her merchandise is good.*[5] Be fully convinced based on solid results that your "merchandise is good." If you want a raise, a promotion, or a new role, you must believe that you deserve it.

Maintain eye contact. Stay powerful in your body language when you are making a request. Maintaining eye contact with the other person makes you appear more authoritative. Failing to look people in the eye conveys weakness and uncertainty.

Practice. As the saying goes, practice makes perfect. The only way to get comfortable and proficient at doing anything is to simply do it. Get into the habit of asking for what you want in general. Tell family members exactly what you want for your birthday. Express your preference for a particular restaurant when planning to eat out with friends. Little wins will prepare you for bigger victories.

Ask the right person. We were taught in geometry that the shortest distance between two points is a straight line. So it is in getting what you want. It is important to go straight to the one who can deliver the goods.

Don't be afraid to ask more than once. We often feel we are bugging people if we have to make a request more than once, but often, people need to hear a message multiple times before they will act. This is particularly important in fundraising or other charitable efforts. You'll want to ask people verbally, via email, and/or via a private post on social media. "For everyone who asks, receives. Everyone who seeks, finds. And to everyone who knocks, the door will be opened."[6] Knocking implies several strikes to a door; stop giving up after a single "hit."

Lessons Learned from the Daughters of Zelophehad

The Bible provides a great example of how to ask for what you want. The Israelites were about to possess the Promised Land. The five daughters of Zelophehad were well aware of the inheritance laws that had been established for allocating the land among various tribes. However, they felt that the laws were unfair, since they prevented them, as women, from inheriting the property owned by their deceased father. They decided to confront Moses and the elders and ask to be exempted. So they called a meeting to present their case:

> They stood before Moses, before Eleazar the priest, and before the leaders and all the congregation, by the doorway of the tabernacle of meeting, saying: "Our father died in the wilderness; but he was not in the company of those who gathered together against the LORD, in company with Korah, but he died in his own sin; and he had no sons. Why should the name of our father be removed

from among his family because he had no son? Give us a possession among our father's brothers."

Moses brought their case before God. And the Lord told Moses,

The daughters of Zelophehad speak what is right; you shall surely give them a possession of inheritance among their father's brothers, and cause the inheritance of their father to pass to them.[7]

These were some assertive women who took matters into their own hands. They had no men in their lives to speak on their behalf— no father, no husbands, no brothers, and no sons. Yes, they had uncles, but it was unlikely that they would support the women in their request, since they were asking for land that would, under the current law, default to the uncles and increase their holdings.

In my book *Confronting Without Offending*, I provide a detailed lesson on the critical lessons that we can learn from their actions.[8] Here are the highlights:

- *Lesson one. They went directly to the one who could effect a change: Moses.*

- *Lesson two. They were very clear as to what they wanted.* They requested their fair share of the land—that is, the same as that allocated to their uncles.

- *Lesson three. They were not deterred by the established law.* They asked to be an exception to it.

- *Lesson four. They made their request on a timely basis.* They were still in the wilderness; the Israelites had not yet conquered the land. Imagine the chaos that would have occurred if the land had to be redistributed after it was already legally allocated. It would be like asking for the promotion after it has already been awarded to Jim.

- *Lesson five. The women were willing to negotiate a win-win settlement.* Just when they thought it safe to "exhale" after their major victory of getting their land request granted, they find that the conflict is not yet over. The uncles later appealed the decision arguing that the new law was now not in their best interest. If the daughters of Zelophehad were to marry outside of their tribe, their land would increase the holdings of their husbands' tribes. Such dilution could not be allowed. God rendered another landmark decision. The Zelophehad Five would have to be flexible and marry within their tribe so that the ancestral property holdings as first allocated would not be diluted. They agreed. "So Zelophehad's daughters did as the LORD commanded Moses. Zelophehad's daughters—Mahlah, Tirzah, Hoglah, Milkah and Noah—married their cousins on their father's side."[9]

- *Lesson six. Their action helped set a new precedent for women's inheritance.* The daughters' courage in asking to be an exception to the law didn't benefit only them. It resulted in a new precedent that benefitted Jewish women for future generations: "And give the following instructions to the people of Israel: If a man dies and has no son, then give his inheritance to his daughters. And if he has no daughter either, transfer his inheritance to his brothers. If he has no brothers, give his inheritance to his father's brothers."[10]

The most obvious consequence of not asking for what you want is that you won't receive whatever it is. The answer will always be no to every unasked request. Here are some other consequences of remaining silent:

- failure to advance to better roles
- lower salary (Men are four times more likely to negotiate and obtain a higher salary. Over the lifetime of your career, you could lose hundreds of thousands of dollars

as annual raises are based on current base salaries. If you are starting at a lower base, your increase will be a lower amount than if computed on a higher base.)

- frustration that you are not where you want to be
- strained relationships because you expect things of people that they know nothing about

---

The answer will always be no to every unasked request.

Asking for what you want can feel totally self-serving, but it actually benefits others as well. When people know what you want or expect, they have the opportunity to give it to you—or not. Don't be afraid to ask for restructured work hours, a change or concession in a company's policy, or other special considerations when you need it—despite the "no-personal-issues-please" mind-set that often prevails in many male-dominated environments. Propose a win-win plan and expect a positive response. In doing so, you just may set a precedent that will improve the quality of life for all women in your environment and your industry.

NEGLECTING TO BUILD A STRONG NETWORK

Networking is a lot like nutrition and fitness. We know what to do, but the hard part is making it a top priority.

Herminia Ibarra, member of the World Economic Forum and Harvard University business professor

If you ask several professional women what they hate most, many of them will say "networking." This is no surprise, as networking tends to make some women feel uncomfortable and inauthentic. Not me. As an extrovert on steroids, I love meeting new people and hearing what they do and how fulfilling they find their work. What I know for sure is that whatever your goals are, they will have to be accomplished through people; failure to network effectively is one of the key obstacles that prevent women from advancing.

Erroneous Beliefs About Networking

Most women hate networking largely because they have certain misconceptions about what it means to network and how it can benefit them. Let's see if I can debunk a few of the myths for you.

You should start with small talk. While it doesn't necessarily hurt to start off talking about family or the weather, it's also perfectly fine to talk about the subject that ties you all together—this is, in most cases, your work. People expect to talk about work; therefore, they won't find it rude or boring if you lead with this in your conversation. You can talk about aspects of your work that you are passionate about and share your professional goals. I love sharing what I do and the various subjects I've written about. When networking, I talk about the message of one of my most popular books (*Confronting Without Offending*) and how people have embraced it at a level that has shocked me. My description of the contents is very brief: "Most people hate conflict, but I teach them that effective confrontation is the key to organizational unity." That's it. I let them ask follow-up questions. If they indicate they'd like to read it, depending on their status, I'll offer to send them a complimentary copy. I make sure to mail it within 48 hours. I never go into a networking event with a WIIFM (What's In It for Me) mind-set soley. If people are interested in following up with me, great. If not, so be it. If I feel I could use their input later, I'll drop them a brief, to-the-point email. Perhaps, this is not the ideal approach, but I find that people are drawn to my enthusiasm and passion.

Networking is mostly a waste of time. Those who lack networking experience often question whether it's a valuable use of their time, especially when the relationships being developed are not immediately related to the task at hand. You must learn to look beyond the act of networking to what you will ultimately gain by building relationships that can later bear fruit.

Some people are just naturally gifted at networking. If you're like most people, you believe networking comes easily for those who are extroverted and runs counter to an introvert's nature. People think like this because they equate being an excellent networker with being the most popular person in the room. However, this is far from the truth. If you see yourself as lacking this "innate" skill, you likely won't invest the time to do it because you don't believe it will get you very far. According to Kuwabara, Hildebrand, and Zou, "If you believe that networking is a skill you can develop you are more likely to be motivated to improve it, work harder at it, and get better returns for your networking than someone with a fixed mindset."[1]

Relationships should form naturally. One of the biggest misconceptions about networking is that relationships should form and grow organically among people who automatically like one another. They feel that working at it strategically and methodically is somehow unethical. However, this way of thinking results in networks that are not useful to you or to your contacts because they are too similar. "Decades of research in social psychology show that left to our own devices we form and maintain relationships with people just like us and with people who are convenient to get to know to because we bump into them often (and if we bump into them often they are more likely to be like us)."[2]

These kinds of networks don't allow for the diversity we need to understand the world around us, make good decisions, and get people who are different from us to embrace our ideas. Therefore, we should develop our professional networks deliberately as part of an intentional effort to cultivate relevant relationships.

Networking is inherently selfish. Many people who fail to engage in networking cite personal values as the reason. They believe networking is an insincere or manipulative way of obtaining an unfair advantage. However, the best networking practices include reciprocity and giving back as much as you receive. The only way to conceive of networking in a more appealing way is to simply experience the value for yourself, for your team, and for your organization. If you think networking is selfish, you probably haven't seen it done correctly.

Familiar, close relationships are the most valuable. Another misconception that gets in the way of successful networking is the idea that our most important relationships are those with people who know us well, our inner circle. While these relationships are certainly important, we often underestimate the importance of relationships with those we don't know well or don't see often. Research shows that these "weaker ties" add "connectivity to our networks by allowing us to reach out to people we don't currently know through the people we do. That's how we learn new things and access far flung information and resources."[3]

Collecting business cards is networking. This is the most common pastime at networking events, and people often feel that once they have handed someone their business card, their networking has been successful. However, the exchange of business cards is useless if it doesn't result in a real connection with the other person. Not only do you want to give people a way to contact you, but you want to give them a reason to *want* to contact you.

Why Network?

Some women believe that networking to socialize and make friends is a positive motive, but networking to enhance their careers is a negative. When I encouraged "Julie," a very talented pastor's wife to engage more in networking, she resisted. "I was taught that it is ungodly to do anything to promote or advantage yourself." Men have known the value of networking since the days of old. Why, if Joseph, the Israelite patriarch, had held this mind-set, he probably would never have been released from the Egyptian jail where he was thrown on false charges. Rather, after interpreting a fellow prisoner's troubling dream, Joseph asked the prisoner (who happened to be the king's cupbearer) to use his influence on his behalf upon being restored to his position. "Please remember me and do me a favor when things go well for you. Mention me to Pharaoh, so he might let me out of this place."[4] This was networking at its best. Joseph showed an interest in the cupbearer's problem, he added value to him by interpreting his dream, and then he asked a favor. Although the cupbearer promptly forgot him, he did remember Joseph's interpretation skills when the king himself had a troubling dream sometime later. Joseph interpreted the dream, put forth a solution to the famine it predicted, and in so doing, became the second most powerful man in all of Egypt. His networking in prison—all orchestrated by the King in Heaven, had paid off.

It is no secret that both men and women benefit from having a network of well-connected peers. During my interview with Shirley Hoogstra (you met her in chapter 20), president of the Council for Christian Colleges and Universities, she reiterated the importance of this reality:

We must encourage women leaders to surround themselves with a constellation of developmental relationships because nobody leads alone. Women leaders need mentors and sponsors who gather around them. God places things in a complementary relationship—meaning, if you're a young leader, get relationships with older leaders. If you're an older leader, make sure that you have a group of peers that encourage you, that can give you advice because you're going to have more and more responsibility. Therefore, you need more and more wisdom.

Women who also have an inner circle of close female contacts are more likely to land executive positions with greater authority and higher pay.[5]

Women often face unconscious bias and other challenges that make it harder for them to advance. Women of color experience special challenges in the workplace when it comes to networking. They are often expected to "dim their light" in the workplace and at networking events to make others feel more comfortable around them. Black women are encouraged to smile more and to not "look so serious." Some are encouraged to carefully time their input so that they don't appear to be too aggressive.

"We must encourage women leaders to surround themselves with a constellation of developmental relationships because nobody leads alone." *Shirley Hoogstra*

Overcoming Your Reluctance to Network

Studies have shown that an aversion to networking can be overcome in the following ways:

1. *Focus on common interests.* Relationships are powerful when they move beyond generic introductions. People

don't normally attend networking events with people with whom they have nothing in common. Such events often have a purpose, which ties the attendees together in some way. Therefore, you can focus on what you might have in common with others to alleviate anxiety and have ready-made topics of discussion to fill in those awkward silences.

I subtly let people know the movers and shakers that I'm friends with but not in a braggadocious way. For example, I might say, "I served on the board of *X* organization with Fred Fat Cat (someone he surely knows), and he added a lot of value to our strategic discussions. I love picking his brain." In this way, the focus is not directly on me but plants the thought *She has a relationship with Fred Fat Cat and that gives her credibility by association.* Some people may call this "playing the game," but I call it "knowing what time it is"—meaning that the time has not yet come in our culture where a woman can boldly mention her achievements and key associations without being viewed as arrogant.

2. *Evaluate what you can give.* Focus on the value you can bring to others rather than on any discomfort you may feel at being in a roomful of strangers making small talk. "When people believe they have a lot to offer others, such as wise advice, mentorship, access, and resources, networking feels easier and less selfish."[6]

3. *Cultivate and nurture relationships.* The real connecting begins after the networking event. Look for ways to establish and nurture a mutually beneficial relationship. For starters, consider following the person on social media and making positive comments on their posts. If you have met an author, purchase their book online and write an Amazon or other review. Find ways to serve the person in a manner that keeps you on their radar screen.

4. *Consider the benefits.* When you attend a networking event, imagine the accomplishments and advancements you will experience if you connect with the right person. Your next opportunity may be only one conversation away. When you have this mind-set about networking, you approach it with excitement, curiosity, and an open mind about all the possibilities that might unfold. You see it as an opportunity for discovery and learning rather than a chore.[7]

You will get the best out of networking when you change your mind-set about it. Embrace the benefits and strategies provided in this chapter. To overcome your aversion, remind yourself that networking "leads to more job and business opportunities, broader and deeper knowledge, improved capacity to innovate, faster advancement, and greater status and authority. Building and nurturing professional relationships also improves the quality of work and increases job satisfaction."[8]

A final word of caution: As you go racing up the achievement ladder, don't forget to network down the ladder also. Don't underestimate the power of the gatekeepers—the administrative assistants, clerks, and others who enjoy a closer relationship than anyone else with their powerful bosses. I received my first book deal with my current publisher after an initial rejection when the assistant to the director of acquisitions insisted they take another look at the manuscript for *30 Days to Taming Your Tongue.* The book went on to sell more than a million copies. In every place that I have ever worked, without ulterior motives, I have made it a point to befriend security guards, secretaries/assistants, and other nonexecutive personnel. They have rewarded me with information and favor I could never have gotten otherwise.

MISUNDERSTANDING THE MALE MIND-SET

*The only difference between men and women is
everything, and that's what keeps things interesting.*

April White, author of *Waging Wars*

When Adam and Eve ate the forbidden fruit, their punishment was swift and severe. Not only were they banished from the Garden of Eden, but the dynamics of their relationship took a sharp turn. God told Eve, "You will desire to control your husband, but he will rule over you."[1] From this point on, sin took its toll on human nature and with it came gender inequality and the battle of the sexes. We have sought and often failed to understand each other and what it takes to navigate the roadblocks associated with walking hand in hand whether at home or in the workplace.

The Male Factor at Home

The discussion that follows focuses on the domestic challenges of being a leader and a wife. If you are single and plan to marry someday, you will appreciate the heads-up. My now-deceased mentor, Dr. Juanita Smith, often said, "Your mate determines your fate." Her admonition to choose carefully was advice worth heeding. As you become more empowered, you will make more money and the demands of managing your success will increase exponentially. Your biggest challenge may be on the home front. Your husband may or may not embrace your ambition or calling. Your income may exceed his. The extent to which you can successfully navigate these issues will depend on your wise communication, negotiation, and navigation.

It can be tough on a husband when his wife has a high-profile, demanding job and he holds a lesser position. Onlookers may erroneously assume that she has a controlling personality and a host of other negative attributes ascribed to high-achieving women. They further assume that he is passive, unambitious, and just going along for the ride. A few may go as far as referring to him as "Mr. Mary" (wife's name). Refinery29 (a popular media and entertainment firm) and Chase Bank conducted a study of couples in which the wife was the high achiever. They found that where the wife was the primary breadwinner, the couple was 15 percent "less likely to identify their marriage as 'very happy'" and 46 percent "more likely to have discussed separation in the past year" than the marriages where the man was the primary breadwinner. But perhaps the most interesting data about female breadwinners was how they felt about it—and how they thought their husbands felt. Almost 50 percent of the female breadwinners thought their husbands felt embarrassed and emasculated by their status.[2]

Beyond the issue of their financial imbalance, a leading woman is usually faced with how to divide domestic responsibilities and how to stroke her husband's ego to assuage his sense of inadequacy. If these issues have caused tension in your relationship, here are a few strategies from our marriage workbook *Financial Intimacy for Couples* that my husband and I have found effective in dealing with such challenges:

1. *Agree on financial priorities.* Most money fights are not due to scarcity of resources but rather a couple's failure to concur on their short-term and long-term goals. While this step requires cooperation, a wife's wise navigation here is critical. Since we tend to be more detail oriented, we can bring specific suggestions to the table for mutual

consideration. For example, you may propose a short-term goal of accumulating at least three to six months of living expenses in an emergency fund, and a long-term goal of paying off your mortgage by the time one of you reaches 60 or retirement age.

2. *Adopt a oneness mind-set toward household income.* I learned the hard way that the greatest path to financial peace in marriage is to adopt the mind-set that everything that comes into the marriage belongs to the marriage. Because I grew up seeing so many financially unempowered women— including my mother—by the time I met my husband, I had developed a selfish "mine-versus-yours" attitude. I had self-financed my college education and secured a lucrative job after graduation. I had no intention of sharing my income with a man. Thanks to great mentoring and an unexpected financial crisis during the first year of our marriage, I was forced to adopt a new way of thinking that left me more than willing to share. Today, even though we maintain different bank accounts for convenience and function, we view all our resources as one.

3. *Ask your husband for specific domestic support.* In many households, even when the woman is the primary breadwinner, she is still expected to fulfill the traditional role of preparing meals and performing other domestic duties. Rather than asking for help, she may fume, fret, and complain that her husband "should" know that she needs more support. Instead of making assumptions, try making a list of all the major tasks required to run your household efficiently. Discuss and negotiate which of you will perform each. Be flexible; traditional gender roles may need to be reversed based on who is most suited or skilled to perform them. The most important thing is to stay in agreement. For your own sanity, abandon perfectionism and learn to be okay

when your husband's proficiency at doing a task is not equal to yours. The world will not stop because he didn't do it your way.

4. *Applaud your husband's contributions big or small.* Yes, he *should* carry a fair share of domestic and other responsibilities, but it's human nature to be even more motivated to continue and even excel the effort by praise and appreciation. If he supports your career and calling, thank him for doing so. Studies show that the majority of women who hold high-profile positions enjoy the support of a faithful husband. Recognize and acknowledge this gift often.

5. *Affirm to your husband regularly that your marriage is more important than your career.* Better yet, demonstrate it is by how you prioritize your time and the energy you put into what makes it work. Miss America 1980, Cheryl Prewitt Salem, has done a magnificent job in this area. When I interviewed her, she shared her story of navigating the male factor at home and professionally.

Me: Cheryl, it sounds like you got over the awesomeness of being Miss America pretty quickly and realized that the title gave you a platform for ministry. You and your husband now minister together. How do you navigate that?

Cheryl: I was ten years into my ministry when my husband, who was a strong man on his own merits, leading Dr. Oral Roberts' ministry for 18 years as his right-hand man with extensive responsibilities, felt the call of God to join me. We formed Salem Family Ministries—which is what I had been praying for. However, I did not realize that I would have to redefine my entire role. I was used to doing it by myself. I was used to coming home and taking off my leadership hat and putting on my mama hat, my wife hat, and my-submission-to-being-number-two   hat.   But when it came to the pulpit and what we do, I had to readjust my thinking and understand that every position God has put me in has always been for his glory. This would be no different. Since I was used to preaching by myself, I would always have something to say. My husband would be talking, and I wouldn't even be listening. All I would be thinking about was what I was going to say next. The Lord began to teach me. He said, "I want you to ask me if you need to say that before you speak. You're never going to be at a loss for something to say or something to reveal. You and your husband are going to pull from each other's anointing. So just because you have a thought, doesn't mean it is necessary for you to share it.

"It's important to let your husband lead. God set order on purpose. Everything in the kingdom of heaven is on purpose, including marriage. It wasn't that the woman couldn't lead, it was that we have a vital and specific role. 'Help meet' means his other side, his other view. It means his front, his back, and all around. We are to go in front when we need to, come behind when we need to, surround him when we need to, be his other side—as needed."

Wise words from a happily married wise woman.

The Male Factor at Work

Let's face it; men wrote the rules for leadership. Many men—and women—despite all the strides that women have made, still believe that leadership is a man's domain. Most books urge us to get in step with this reality lest we get emotionally and professionally stuck bemoaning how unfair it is. Well, that's not a bad idea; however, things are changing, albeit at a slower pace than we desire. Women who want to fast-track their journey to gender equality must consider the advantage of learning the professional rules of engagement in order to work with men effectively. Below are some key truths and observations that I believe women need to understand about the male factor at work based on what I've learned over four decades of corporate and nonprofit leadership.

Many men—and women—despite all the strides that women have made, still believe that leadership is a man's domain.

- *Understand what men mean when they say, "It's not personal, it's just business."* Most men make a distinction between their personal lives and their professional lives; they generally believe the two should not overlap. Based on that mind-set, they are frustrated when women get emotional or feel rejected about a negative evaluation or a disappointment. On the other hand, women don't separate their lives into two different buckets. And for better or worse, their personal and professional issues often compete for top priority. When you face a situation that your superior has explained as "just business," step back and try to see the business advantage of it. If you can't, seek to understand by simply asking for an explanation. "Just for clarity, can you explain the business advantage here?"

- *Don't hesitate to ask for help.* You don't have to present your request like a damsel in distress or pretend that you know everything. Most men enjoy the satisfaction of rescuing women whether it is lifting heavy objects or sharing their knowledge. Be vulnerable but also be confident in what you know. Be mature enough to acknowledge what you don't know or can't do.

- *Don't circle the airport when explaining a problem or its proposed solution.* Men tend to want the short version of a story so that they will know what action to take based on the information you are providing. Thus it is wise to give them the bottom line first. This will earn you high marks in their eyes because you understand that time is money and that you must use it efficiently in communicating.

- *Learn to talk sports; it can make you more relatable—and can lead to your being included more often.* Listen to sports talk radio shows or podcasts during drive times to keep abreast of the latest news. You don't need to know all the details of the latest superstar's contract but just enough to ask intelligent questions. Now, you are probably thinking, "Are men going to seek ways to be more relatable with us?" Probably not, but this book is about your individual efforts to proactively forge your path to gender equality. Their behavior is outside of your control.

- *Don't talk about personal "female issues."* When you discuss female surgeries, nuances of pregnancy, and so forth with men, they deem such subjects unprofessional or inappropriate.

- *Get along with other women as best you can.* Men hate having to referee a "catfight"—which is any conflict between two women, as far as they are concerned. Rather than intervening, I've seen them bury their heads in the sand and let the conflict brew forever or fire the one they are most prepared to do without. That could be you!

- *Don't volunteer for stereotypical "women's work."* Getting coffee or picking up lunch may be a great way to become more likable, but it won't earn you any leadership points. I'm not a coffee drinker and even during the early days of my career, I never learned to make it lest I get stuck with this entrenched gender role. Of course, if sharing the

duty with your male colleagues is the norm in your environment, then make the coffee when it's your turn.

- *Don't put a man in the awkward position of trying not to
  notice your cleavage, your skintight outfit, or other allur-
  ing attire.* Dress for credibility and respect. (See the
  discussion on executive presence in chapter 20.) If a
  man attempts to cross the line and sexually harass you,
  respond strongly the first time it happens: "Hold up, no
  trespassing! We all need our jobs!" If he tries it again, have
  the courage to report it. *Caution:* Don't send mixed signals by casually flirting with him and then rejecting his
  subsequent advances.

- *Don't be super sensitive by looking for gender discrimination
  under every rock.* The safer you are to talk to, the more
  likely men will listen to you when there is a legitimate,
  documentable issue that needs to be brought to their
  attention.

If this list sounds like we must tailor our professional behavior to the historical preferences of most men, know that these are
not *commands* but *cautions* that could help advance your ball down
the court faster if you understand them. Shaunti Feldhahn, social
researcher and businesswoman, reports the findings of her extensive
and enlightening study of men's mind-sets in the workplace in her
book *The Male Factor.* I highly recommend it for a more detailed discussion of the nuances of working with men.

EPILOGUE

In this book, we have concentrated our discussion on your individual quest for gender equality as an authentic woman who knows and values what she brings to the table. Yes, men have had the advantage since the beginning of time, but times are changing. Our goal now is not to gain the upper hand but to learn to walk hand in hand with them. We need each other to be fruitful, to be profitable. It is God's way.

I pray that you have resolved not to sacrifice a single iota of femininity in order to be an effective leader. God has equipped you with innate traits that will allow you to excel. Don't run from being collaborative, emotionally savvy, nurturing, communicative, intuitive, motivational, resilient, persistent, flexible, vulnerable, servant-hearted, principled, and resourceful. These are your weapons against gender inequality. Use them, sharpen them, manage them and watch yourself soar. And yes, you can have it all—all that God has ordained. Just be sure that your definition of "all" is in alignment with his. For this season of my life, here is what my "all" looks like.

- maintaining spiritual disciplines, such as prayer and reading the Scriptures
- spending quality time with my husband and maintaining a weekly "date night"
- being the childless matriarch of a huge family and keeping them connected via a weekly conference prayer call

- writing books that challenge people to apply the Scriptures to their lives

- speaking to live audiences and making media appearances to reinforce my core message: practical application of God's Word will make you a winner in every major pillar of your life

- engaging with a very limited number of financial clients to help them with financial reporting and accountability

- staying connected to old friends via periodic lunch/dinner dates

- finding time to stroll and window-shop at my favorite outdoor mall

- occasionally binging on old sitcoms that make me laugh out loud

Are there more activities or projects that I'd like to add to this list? You bet, but God will have to show me what to let go of or what to reduce my involvement in so that I can maintain a work-life balance. I loved hosting and coproducing my own faith-based TV show *Winning with Deborah* for a couple of seasons on the *TBN Salsa Network*, however, it was grueling work. To resume, I would have to go back to my prayer closet and answer the "why" questions that help me properly prioritize my time. I want to make sure that my motivation for doing anything is God-honoring versus ego-gratifying. I'd also love to engage in formal group mentoring, but I choose to maintain a flexible schedule to accommodate my husband's impromptu adventures and to enjoy other quality-of-life activities during this season of my life. Yes, I want it *all*—God's *all*. He must be pleased with my priorities.

Let's not be disheartened by the projection that it will take another 200 years to achieve gender equality. God has never been restricted by statistical projections, traditional mind-sets, or cultural norms. Stay optimistic about your individual journey but never stop looking for ways and opportunities to add value to other sisters pursuing their destiny.

Tap into your innate traits and quiz yourself often regarding how effectively you are using them. Ask yourself, *"Am I tapping into the assets I've already been given?" "Am I taking a trait to an extreme so that it has now become a liability?" "Do I need to make a correction?"* Periodically review the 12 counterproductive tendencies and ask yourself, "Am I exhibiting this behavior?" "What step can I take right now to begin eliminating it?"

Finally, don't forget to express sincere appreciation to and for the men who have been your mentors up close or remotely—as well as the unofficial/official sponsors who have used their influence to open doors. My deepest gratitude goes to Bishop Charles Blake, head of West Angeles Church, the famed megachurch whose members include numerous Hollywood A-listers, for hiring me as chief financial officer and trusting me to negotiate the best possible bank financing deal for the construction of their famed cathedral. It was a landmark transaction and a life-changing, nine-year experience. Bishop Edward Smith, through his dynamic faith teaching and personal prodding, challenged me more than two decades ago to pursue my passion for writing and speaking. He later recommended me for my very first board of director's seat with a major multimillion-dollar nonprofit. This led to seats on other high-profile boards that have changed the trajectory of my life. Hollywood filmmaker and media consultant to megaministries Dr. Phil Cooke has been an incredible mentor with invaluable advice and coaching on managing the media aspects of my career. His generosity with his time has been amazing. Dr. Leith Anderson, former president of the National Association of Evangelicals, in a single mentoring session helped me determine how to merge my love for the Scriptures, my corporate and business experience, and my passion to see women excel in confidence and leadership into a powerful ministry. John Jenkins, pastor of the renowned, award-winning First Baptist Church of Glenarden (Maryland), is one of the most generous, humble, and down-to-earth men I have ever met. The support from him and his wife, Trina, launched my writing career. They continue to convince me that I am surrounded with the favor of God. Terry Glaspey, director of acquisitions for Harvest House Publishers, has been a great source of inspiration and motivation for "the next book"; he always has an encouraging word, a practical approach, and a positive solution to my writing challenges. I'm eternally grateful for all these men who embrace gender equality in word and deed. Most of all, I'm beyond thankful for my husband, Darnell. None of what I do would be possible without his unwavering love, prayers, boundaries, patience, and support.

Are there any men that you need to stop and appreciate? They are your evidence of God's blessings on your leadership. He has surrounded you with favor,[1] and no one can thwart your divine destiny. Don't believe the lie that all men marginalize women. Most want you to succeed and to engage with them as respected equals. So lead, ladies…lead with your inherent female traits…lead like a woman!

WORDS OF WISDOM FROM WINNING WOMEN

Below are brief statements of wisdom I collected from a select group of women whom I know up close and personally. Their views, convictions, and example have enriched my life spiritually, physically, relationally, emotionally, and financially.

On Seeking God's Guidance...

God is looking for women who will walk in their kingdom authority by boldly acting on His promises. Don't allow past setbacks, disappointments, or any other negative experiences to stop you from pursuing the positive future He has planned for you. Learn to view every adversity as a growth experience and always make seeking His guidance a daily priority. He will reward you with the wisdom and the courage to lead with excellence—for His glory.

Dr. Barbara McCoo Lewis, General Supervisor of Women, Church of God in Christ International

On Perpetual Learning...

Over the last 10 years, women and men have increasingly asked to "pick my brain." It's really interesting because when I respond to their questions, I realize I've learned a lot of lessons. When people pick my brain, I learn also. So always be learning, be humble, be curious—and raise your hand.

Jo Anne Lyon, former General Superintendent of the Wesleyan Church (first woman elected), founder of World Hope International

On Distractions and Determination...

I had several distractions, detours, and delays—including having children—before I was able to fully pursue my first passion: theatrical acting. The balance of work and home responsibilities often continues to deter women from pursuing artistic and business endeavors. However, my dad, a basketball coach, often inspired me with these words from his mentor, former UCLA coach John Wooden, "Do not let what you cannot do interfere with what you can do." My dad taught me to be persistent and not to be deterred by interruptions. My Heavenly Father has also taught me that when you are pursuing what you are called to do.

> **Kathleen Cooke,** cofounding partner at Cooke Media Group,
> cofounder of the Influence Lab, author of *Hope 4 Today:*
> *Stay Connected to God in a Distracted Culture*

On Knowing Who You Are...

To be successful in navigating through the difficult challenge stemming from isolation, negative judgment, tokenism, and other roadblocks, I found that if you have a strong spiritual, mental, and physical regimen, you can navigate any situation. It starts with courage and knowing that you are the head and not the tail. However, women need to understand that they need to focus on hard tasks and understanding the business. Soft jobs, staff jobs, do not get you to the C-suite.

> **Joan Robinson-Berry,** vice president/chief engineer,
> Boeing Global Services (first African American woman
> chief engineer in the aerospace industry)

On Comparing, Competing, and Coveting...

Whenever you let others define you and your essence, you block your progress to thriving in your own uniqueness. So beware of comparing, competing, and coveting in your interactions with other women, for these habits are a sure path to depression, discouragement, and discontentment. Someone else's greatness takes nothing from your distinction. Just because you are not the best at something does not mean that you can't be a success. Embrace your uniqueness and do the best with what God has given you.

Cheryl Martin, former news anchor, speaker, author of
*Distinctly You: Trading Comparison & Competition
for Freedom & Fulfillment*

On Emotional Rest…

Emotional rest, pouring out in this area has a lot to do with people-pleasing behaviors. So the pouring out is saying the yeses when you really should say no because you don't really want to do it. You're giving a reluctant yes rather than a truthful no. And what happens with that is you start letting go of your personal boundaries and then you start feeling devalued because people are stepping in on your boundary. But you didn't really erect them in a way that they even know that they're doing something you're not happy with. And so, reclaiming that emotional rest begins with taking ownership of your nos and feeling that level of comfort to just be authentic. When something isn't a good fit for you, you have the freedom to say that without having to explain it to anyone.

Sandra Dalton-Smith, MD, *Good Housekeeping* top-100 medical
expert, author of *Sacred Rest: Recover Your Life, Renew Your Energy,
Restore Your Sanity*

On Maintaining Good Health…

Women in leadership must understand that their health is their true wealth. Without optimum health in mind, body, and spirit, a woman cannot lead a team, run a company, or even a household for that matter at their fullest potential. The ripple effect of great health is increase and abundance in every area of your life. Invest in your health and you will reap unlimited dividends.

Wendie Pett, host of *Visibly Fit,*
creator of the Visibly Fit Wellness Program

On Hispanic Women Overcoming Cultural Barriers...

In a 2013 survey conducted by the Pew Research Center, two-thirds of Hispanics said that our community needs a leader. I found these results interesting as they highlight a narrow understanding of leadership that has overtaken our culture. Leadership is not about who is on television or who is at the microphone and on the stage, but it is about that individual who serves. Our heritage is full of *abuelitas, tias*, and mothers who despite a myriad of challenges found ways to make sure their children were clothed and fed and were fully equipped to go pursue all that life had to offer. Because of these leaders in our homes, many of us have more opportunities to lead not only in our home but in the larger community. For many of us, however, we are inhibited from engaging to lead in multicultural contexts. Our fear of not fitting in, of not understanding the context of others, or of being shamed because our experience is different from others prevents us from stepping into different ethnic contexts in which we can learn and, importantly, others can learn from us. Know that when you were born into a Hispanic family, God knew what He was doing. It wasn't to put you into a place of shame or fear but to show off another dimension of who He is. There is no need to be afraid. Know that because you are Hispanic, you have something to offer to the God-purposed and designed mosaic of His kingdom. Step in and lead the way!

Lisa Trevino Cummins, president of Urban Strategies, LLC,
coauthor of *Inheritance: Discovering the Richness of Latino
Family and Culture*

On Finishing Strong...

When a woman knows she has the calling of God upon her life, she wisely spends time in preparation. She learns to listen to the voice of the Spirit and to become obedient in the smallest areas. There is no room for excuses or for blaming others.

There is a Chinese proverb that says, "When sleeping women wake, mountains move." We are seeing the prophetic promise of Psalm 68 come to pass: "The Lord gives the word of power; the women who bear and publish the good news are a great host." It's our season to make great strides in gender equality. When adversity, personal sorrow, and hardship occur, the anointing enables a godly woman to finish her race strong. As for me, I never accept no as the final answer. If I believe God is directing my path, I am willing to do whatever it takes to finish strong.

Frieda C. White, humanitarian and author of
A Woman God Can Use

A Final Word from Me on Being Financially Savvy…

As your spending power increases, you must become more financially astute, gaining the wisdom that you need to make informed decisions. This requires getting a foundational understanding of the financial jargon, concepts, and strategies that will empower you to engage in personal and business transactions with confidence and peace. Be quick to invest in your learning and development. You will indeed develop a "head for figures" when you increase your knowledge and make God the head of your life.

Excerpted and adapted from Deborah Smith Pegues,
The One-Minute Money Mentor for Women (Harvest House, 2018)

NOTES

Prologue

1. "Men or Women: Who's the Better Leader?," *Pew Research Center*, August 25, 2008, http://www.pewsocialtrends.org/2008/08/25/men-or-women-whos-the-better-leader.

2. "Women CEOs of the S&P 500," *Catalyst*, October 4, 2019, http://www.catalyst.org/research/women-ceos-of-the-sp-500.

Chapter 1: Collaborative

1. Carolyn Gregoire, "The Giving Habits of Americans May Surprise You," *HuffPost*, last updated December 6, 2017, http://www.huffpost.com/entry/are-you-a-giver-huffpost-_n_3785215.

Chapter 2: Emotionally Savvy

1. Risto Siilasmaa, "What Role Should Emotions Play in Developing Strategies in Business and Life?" *Quora*, November 15, 2018, http://www.quora.com/What-role-should-emotions-play-in-developing-strategies-in-business-and-life/answer/Risto-Siilasmaa-1.

2. See 1 Samuel 24.

3. Proverbs 19:11 NIV.

Chapter 3: Nurturing

1. Gabrielle Anagnostopoulos, "Follow This Leader: Ava DuVernay," *The Howl*, Queen's Commerce Leadership Summit, August 22, 2017, http://www.qcleadershipsummit.com/single-post/2017/08/22/Follow-This-Leader-Ava-DuVernay.

2. Mark Mann, as quoted in "What Is Pruning? The Importance, Benefits and Methods of Pruning," *Davey* (blog), September 12, 2018, http://blog.davey.com/2018/09/what-is-pruning-the-importance-benefits-and-methods-of-pruning.

Chapter 4: Communicative

1. Genesis 11:1-9.

2. Anchal Luthra and Richa Dahiya, "Effective Leadership Is All About Communicating Effectively: Connecting Leadership and Communication," *International Journal of Management and Business Studies* 5, no. 3 (2015): 44, http://www.mcgill.ca/engage/files/engage/effective_leadership_is_all_about_communicating_effectively_luthra_dahiya_2015.pdf.

3. "Why Communication Is So Important for Leaders," *Center for Creative Leadership*, http://www.ccl.org/articles/leading-effectively-articles/communication-1-idea-3-facts-5-tips.

4. 1 Corinthians 2:4-5.

5. Mark 4:33-34.

6. Carol Kinsey Goman, "Are There Gender Differences in Workplace Communication?," *LinkedIn*, July 20, 2017, http://www.linkedin.com/pulse/gender-differences-workplace-communication-carol-kinsey-goman-ph-d-.

7. Tim Sackett, "What Over Communicating Says About You," *The Tim Sackett Project* (blog), June 6, 2011, http://timsackett.com/2011/06/06/what-over-communicating-says-about-you.

8. Andra Picincu, "The Advantages of Effective Communication Skills," *Bizfluent*, last updated November 2, 2018, http://bizfluent.com/list-6651408-advantages-effective-communication-skills.html.

9. Censuswide and Geckoboard, Research Report, "'Mushroom Management' Leaves Employees Heading for the Door," September 2015, https://www.entrepreneur.com/article/274279.

Chapter 5: Intuitive

1. Amy K. Stanton, "Why I Trust My Intuition 100% of the Time as a Female Founder—and Why You Should, Too," *Hacker Noon*, September 20, 2018, http://hackernoon.com/why-i-trust-my-intuition-100-of-the-time-as-a-female-founder-and-why-you-should-too-21298206a692.

2. Job 38:36.

3. John Townsend, *Leadership Beyond Reason: How Great Leaders Succeed by Harnessing the Power of Their Values, Feelings, and Intuition* (Nashville: Thomas Nelson, 2009), xvii.

4. Proverbs 16:25.

Chapter 6: Motivational

1. "State of the American Manager," *Gallup*, http://www.gallup.com/services/182138/state-american-manager.aspx.

2. "State of the American Manager."

3. Adam Grant, *Give and Take: Why Helping Others Drives Our Success* (New York: Penguin, 2014), 168.

4. Tom Rath and Donald O. Clifton, *How Full Is Your Bucket?* (New York: Gallup, 2009), 17.

5. Eric Geiger, "Seven Differences Between Motivating and Manipulating," *Eric Geiger* (blog), May 17, 2016, http://ericgeiger.com/2016/05/seven-differences-between-motivating-and-manipulating.

6. Harvey Schachter, "What Motivates Employees? It's Not Just the Money," *The Globe and Mail*, July 15, 2013, last updated May 11, 2018, http://www.theglobeandmail.com/report-on-business/careers/management/what-motivates-employees-its-not-just-the-money/article13205253.

7. Faisal Hoque, "Three Habits of Motivational Leaders," *Fast Company*, October 22, 2015, http://www.fastcompany.com/3052188/three-habits-of-motivational-leaders.

Chapter 7: Resilient/Persistent: Bouncing Back and Moving Forward

1. Maya Angelou, *Letter to My Daughter* (New York: Random House, 2008), xii.

2. Job 14:1 NKJV.

3. F. R. H. Zijlstra , M. Cropley, & L. W. Rydstedt, SPECIAL ISSUE PAPER, "From Recovery to Regulation: An Attempt to Reconceptualize 'Recovery from Work' Introduction," *Stress and Health* 30: 244-252 (2014), https://www.academia.edu/7904615/SPECIAL_ISSUE_PAPER_From_Recovery_to_Regulation_An_Attempt_to_Reconceptualize_Recovery_from_Work_Introduction.

4. Zijlstra, Cropley, & Rydstedt, "From Recovery to Regulation."

5. Arianna Huffington, *The Sleep Revolution: Transforming Your Life, One Night at a Time* (New York: Harmony, 2017), 23.

6. William Arthur Ward, *Thoughts of a Christian Optimist: The Words of William Arthur Ward* (Anderson, SC: Droke House, 1968), 55.

Chapter 8: Flexible

1. "State of the American Manager," *Gallup*, http://www.gallup.com/services/182138/state-american-manager.aspx.

2. Kirsten Blakemore Edwards, "Five Stories from Trailblazing Women Leaders," *Inc.*, September 19,

2018, http://www.inc.com/partners-in-leadership/5-stories-from-high-impact-women-leaders. html.

3. Susan Wojcicki, as quoted in Jonathan Mahler, "YouTube's Chief, Hitting a New 'Play' Button," *The New York Times*, December 20, 2014, http://www.nytimes.com/2014/12/21/business/youtubes-chief-hitting-a-new-play-button.html.

4. Nicole Lipkin, "Unintended Consequences of Being Too Flexible as a Leader," *Equilibria* (blog), August 7, 2017, http://equilibrialeadership.com/blog/unintended-consequences-of-being -too-flexible-as-a-leader.

5. Liz Bywater, "The Flexible Leader: An Adaptable Approach to Managing Your Team," News, Advice and Insight, *WJM Associates*, April 2012, http://www.wjmassoc.com/insight/the -flexible-leader.

6. Bywater, "The Flexible Leader."

Chapter 9: Vulnerable

1. Gregory Lewis, "Why Being Vulnerable at Work Can Be Your Biggest Advantage, According to Brené Brown," *LinkedIn Talent Blog*, October 4, 2017, http://business.linkedin.com/talent -solutions/blog/talent-connect/2017/why-being-vulnerable-at-work-can-be-your-biggest -advantage-according-to-brene-brown.

2. Brené Brown, as quoted in Lewis, "Being Vulnerable at Work."

Chapter 10: Servant-Hearted

1. Robert K. Greenleaf, *The Power of Servant-Leadership*, ed. Larry C. Spears (San Francisco: Berrett -Koehler, 1998), 123.

2. Luke 22:24-26.

3. Marcel Schwantes, "The World's Ten Top CEOs (They Lead in a Totally Unique Way)," *Inc.*, March 29, 2017, http://www.inc.com/marcel-schwantes/heres-a-top-10-list-of-the-worlds-best -ceos-but-they-lead-in-a-totally-unique-wa.html.

4. Marcel Schwantes, "This Popular Female CEO's Leadership Style May End the Debate on Best Leadership Style," *Inc.*, February 17, 2017, http://www.inc.com/marcel-schwantes/this-popular -female-ceos-leadership-style-may-end-the-debate-on-best-leadership-.html.

5. Schwantes, "The World's Ten Top CEOs."

6. J. Oswald Sanders, *Spiritual Leadership: A Commitment to Excellence for Every Believer* (Chicago, IL: Moody, 2007), 13.

7. John R. Stott, https://quotefancy.com/quote/1432493/John-R-W-Stott-Leaders-have-power -but-power-is-safe-only-in-the-hands-of-those-who-humble-themselves-to-serve.

Chapter 11: Principled

1. Laura Kray, as quoted in Shankar Vedantam, interview by David Greene, "Why Men Outnumber Women Attending Business Schools," *Hidden Brain* (podcast transcript), *NPR*, April 9, 2014, http://www.npr.org/2014/04/09/300836825/why-men-outnumber-women-attending-business -schools.

2. Colossians 3:23 NKJV.

3. Andrea Learned, "Do Women Have Stronger Ethical Business Principles than Men?," *The Guardian*, May 15, 2014, http://www.theguardian.com/sustainable-business/women-stronger-ethical -business-men.

Chapter 12: Resourceful

1. Judges 9:54 NKJV. Read the story in verses 49-54.

2. Glenn Llopis, "The Most Undervalued Leadership Traits of Women," *Forbes*, February 3, 2014, http://www.forbes.com/sites/glennllopis/2014/02/03/the-most-undervalued-leadership-traits-of-women/#2cf1984d38a1.

3. Sherrie Campbell, "Six Characteristics of Resourceful People That Bring Them Success," *Entrepreneur*, March 10, 2016, http://www.entrepreneur.com/article/272171.

4. John Wooden and Jay Carty, *Coach Wooden's Pyramid of Success: Building Blocks for a Better Life* (Grand Rapids, MI: Revell, 2015), 106.

5. Craig Impelman, "Why Resourcefulness Is an Important Personal Trait," *Success*, September 13, 2017, http://www.success.com/why-resourcefulness-is-an-important-personal-trait.

6. "Estée Lauder Biography," *Biography*, April 2, 2014, last updated August 22, 2019, http://www.biography.com/business-figure/estee-lauder.

7. "Estée Lauder Biography."

8. Proverbs 31:10-31.

Chapter 13: Lacking Confidence

1. Cindy Foster, as quoted in Elizabeth Chuck and Shamar Walters, "Tammie Jo Shults, Who Landed Crippled Southwest Plane, Was One of First Female Fighter Pilots in U.S. Navy," *NBC News*, with contributions from Alex Johnson and *The Associated Press*, April 18, 2018, http://www.nbcnews.com/news/us-news/tammie-jo-shults-who-landed-crippled-southwest-plane-was-one-n866951.

2. Judges 4:8.

Chapter 14: Pursuing Perfection

1. David Viscott, *Emotionally Free: Letting Go of the Past to Live in the Moment* (Chicago, IL: Contemporary, 1992), 54.

Chapter 15: Disfavoring Other Women

1. Howland Blackiston, "Understanding the Role of the Queen Bee in a Hive," *Dummies*, accessed January 16, 2020, http://www.dummies.com/home-garden/hobby-farming/beekeeping/understanding-the-role-of-the-queen-bee-in-a-hive.

2. Anne Perkins, "Margaret Thatcher Obituary," *The Guardian*, April 8, 2013, http://www.theguardian.com/politics/2013/apr/08/margaret-thatcher-political-phenomenon-dies.

3. Louise Doughty, "Historically, Women in Power Out-Men the Men," from an interview by Susanna Rustin, Harriet Gibsone, and Hanna Yusuf, "What If Women Ruled the World?" *The Guardian*, July 5, 2017, http://www.theguardian.com/artanddesign/2017/jul/05/what-if-women-ruled-the-world.

4. Psalm 75:6-7 NKJV.

5. Judges 5:24-27 NKJV.

Chapter 16: Chronic Multitasking

1. "Enjoli Perfume 'I'm a Woman' Commerical (1979)," YouTube video, posted by "Bionic Disco," November 15, 2017, http://www.youtube.com/watch?v=N_kzJ-f5C9U.

2. "Multitasking: Switching Costs," *American Psychological Association*, March 20, 2006, http://www.apa.org/research/action/multitask.

3. "Eight Reasons Why Multitasking Reduces Your Productivity," *Boost* (blog), *Brightpod*, November 7, 2013, http://www.brightpod.com/boost/8-reasons-why-multitasking-reduces-your-productivity.

4. "The Myth of Multitasking Exercise—Revisited," *Dave Crenshaw*, accessed January 16, 2020, http://davecrenshaw.com/myth-of-multitasking-exercise.

5. Dave Crenshaw, "How to Manage Your Time Effectively—Eight Practical Tips," YouTube video, posted by "Dave Crenshaw," September 11, 2018, http://www.youtube.com/watch?v=7xmoU0GsOag.

6. Stéphane Marchand, "The Myth of Multitasking, and Other Inattention Stories," *Paris Innovation Review*, December 11, 2017, http://parisinnovationreview.com/articles-en/the-myth-of-multitasking-and-other-inattention-stories, excerpted from Stéphane Marchand, *Les Secrets de Votre Cerveau* (Paris: Fayard, 2017).

7. Learn more about StayFocusd at http://chrome.google.com/webstore/detail/stayfocusd/laankejkbhbdhmipfmgcngdelahlfoji?hl=en.

8. Learn more about FocusMe at http://focusme.com.

9. Learn more about OffTime at http://offtime.app.

Chapter 17: Downplaying Skills and Accomplishments

1. Proverbs 27:2.

2. Priya Fielding-Singh, Devon Magliozzi, and Swethaa Ballakrishnen, "Why Women Stay Out of the Spotlight at Work," *Harvard Business Review*, August 28, 2018, http://hbr.org/2018/08/why-women-stay-out-of-the-spotlight-at-work.

3. Amy Morin, "Seven Ways to Talk About Your Accomplishments Without Sounding Like a Braggart," *Forbes*, January 29, 2017, http://www.forbes.com/sites/amymorin/2017/01/29/7-ways-to-talk-about-your-accomplishments-without-sounding-like-a-braggart/#3f2d586d6fcc.

4. Sheryl Sandberg, as quoted in an interview by Norah O'Donnell, "Sheryl Sandberg Pushes Women to 'Lean In,'" *60 Minutes* (show script), *CBS News*, March 11, 2013, http://www.cbsnews.com/news/sheryl-sandberg-pushes-women-to-lean-in-11-03-2013.

Chapter 18: Forsaking Work-Life Balance

1. Henry Cloud, "Boundaries That Give You Control of Your Life," *Everyday Answers with Joyce Meyer*, *Joyce Meyer Ministries*, accessed January 16, 2020, http://joycemeyer.org/everydayanswers/ea-teachings/boundaries-that-give-you-control-of-your-life.

2. Tim Kehl, "Twelve Key Strategies to Achieving a Work-Life Balance," *IndustryWeek*, April 18, 2012, http://www.industryweek.com/leadership/article/21982458/12-key-strategies-to-achieving-a-worklife-balance.

Chapter 19: Lacking Executive Presence

1. Shaunti Feldhahn, *The Male Factor: The Unwritten Rules, Misperceptions, and Secret Beliefs of Men in the Workplace* (New York: Crown, 2009), Kindle edition, chapter 10.

2. Adapted from Deborah Smith Pegues, *The One-Minute Money Mentor for Women: 21 Strategies for Financial Empowerment* (Eugene, OR: Harvest House, 2018), 94-98.

Chapter 21: Failing to Engage Constructive Feedback

1. Shelley J. Correll and Caroline Simard, "Research: Vague Feedback Is Holding Women Back," *Harvard Business Review*, April 29, 2016, http://hbr.org/2016/04/research-vague-feedback-is-holding-women-back.

2. Exodus 18:17 NIV.

Chapter 22: Expecting Instead of Asking

1. Sheryl Sandberg and Adam Grant, "Speaking While Female," *The New York Times*, January 12, 2015, https://www.nytimes.com/2015/01/11/opinion/sunday/speaking-while-female.html.

2. KPMG LLP, *KPMG Women's Leadership Study: Moving Women Forward into Leadership Roles*, 2015, accessed January 17, 2020, http://home.kpmg/content/dam/kpmg/ph/pdf/ThoughtLeadershipPublications/KPMGWomensLeadershipStudy.pdf.

3. Linda Babcock and Sara Laschever, *Women Don't Ask: Negotiation and the Gender Divide* (Princeton, NJ: Princeton University, 2003), chap. 4.

4. Linda Babcock, interview by Shellie Karabell, "Why Women Don't Ask," YouTube video, 7:05–8:50, posted by "INSEAD," April 6, 2011, http://www.youtube.com/watch?v=3Rum1YRLDKs.

5. Proverbs 31:18 NKJV.

6. Matthew 7:8.

7. Numbers 27:2-7 NKJV.

8. Adapted from Deborah Smith Pegues, *Confronting Without Offending* (Eugene, OR: Harvest House, 2009), 58-62.

9. Numbers 36:10-11 NIV.

10. Numbers 27:8-10.

Chapter 23: Neglecting to Build a Strong Network

1. Herminia Ibarra, "Five Misconceptions About Networking," *Harvard Business Review*, April 18, 2016, http://hbr.org/2016/04/5-misconceptions-about-networking.

2. Ibarra, "Five Misconceptions About Networking."

3. Ibarra, "Five Misconceptions About Networking."

4. Genesis 40:14.

5. Shelley Zalis, "Power of the Pack: Women Who Support Women Are More Successful," *Forbes*, March 6, 2019, http://www.forbes.com/sites/shelleyzalis/2019/03/06/power-of-the-pack-women-who-support-women-are-more-successful/#278b71561771.

6. Tiziana Casciaro, Francesca Gino, and Maryam Kouchaki, "Learn to Love Networking," *Harvard Business Review*, May 2016, https://hbr.org/2016/05/learn-to-love-networking.

7. Zalis, "Power of the Pack."

8. Casciaro, Gino, and Kouchaki, "Learn to Love Networking."

Chapter 24: Misunderstanding the Male Mind-Set

1. Genesis 3:16.

2. "What the Modern American Family Looks Like—By the Numbers," *Refinery29*, sponsored by Chase Bank, January 17, 2018, http://www.refinery29.com/en-us/women-breadwinners-household-income-family-impact.

Epilogue

1. Psalm 5:12 NIV.

Acknowledgments

There are many, many people whose efforts made this work possible—too many to name, lest I forget someone. So I'll just say thank you; you know who you are. Thank you, God, for your favor in surrounding me with prayer intercessors, researchers, volunteer beta readers, encouraging friends, and women who shared their stories through formal interviews, informal phone calls, text messages, and other means.

Thank you for a great publisher with a great staff. And of course, a special thank you to my awesome, supportive husband, Darnell, my cheerleader and life partner.

May the message of this book bless all who encounter it.

About the Author

Deborah Smith Pegues is a CPA/MBA, certified John Maxwell Leadership Coach and Speaker, certified behavior consultant, Bible teacher, and international speaker. She has written 17 transformational books, including the bestselling *30 Days to Taming Your Tongue* (over one million sold worldwide) and *The One-Minute Money Mentor for Women*. She and her husband, Darnell, have been married 41 years.